BLACK
IN THE
POCKET

AFRICAN AMERICAN QUARTERBACKS
THAT CHANGED THE FACE OF AMERICAN FOOTBALL

TOM COLE

authorHOUSE®

AuthorHouse™
1663 Liberty Drive
Bloomington, IN 47403
www.authorhouse.com
Phone: 833-262-8899

Published by AuthorHouse 07/15/2024

ISBN: 979-8-8230-2828-8 (sc)
ISBN: 979-8-8230-2827-1 (e)

Library of Congress Control Number: 2024911553

Print information available on the last page.

Any people depicted in stock imagery provided by Getty Images are models, and such images are being used for illustrative purposes only.
Certain stock imagery © Getty Images.

This book is printed on acid-free paper.

Because of the dynamic nature of the Internet, any web addresses or links contained in this book may have changed since publication and may no longer be valid. The views expressed in this work are solely those of the author and do not necessarily reflect the views of the publisher, and the publisher hereby disclaims any responsibility for them.

Contents

Dedication

Dedicated to all the African American Quarterbacks
that persevered and struggled in the 1960's, 1970's
and 1980's to create a level and fairer playing field that
exists today in Pro Football for Black Quarterbacks.

So, a ten-year-old Black youngster in his backyard throwing a
football through a tire hanging from a tree limb can not only dream
of being a Pro Quarterback but can do it. The struggle was real.

The Deception

In the 1950's, 1960's and 1970's why weren't more African American athletes playing the quarterback position in high school and college in the United States. It is a question that needs to be vetted.

In full disclosure I was raised by a mother, Joanne Cole, who taught me that you never looked at someone of color differently. I was privileged to coach high school and college football for 20 years, from 1974 to 1994. I truly never thought about race when I called for quarterbacks. Those that came to my part of the field I coached. I truly never thought of Black, White or Brown. But I did hear a different discourse from many coaches. The African American quarterback will want to run not stay in the pocket. "Maybe they won't work as hard to learn the playbook." "Could they lead the team?" All completely ridiculous concepts and thoughts. Those coaches should have asked my mom. She would have told them. There were always subtle and not-so-subtle comments. Black kids that wanted to play quarterback would be better off playing, as some completely uninformed coaches have said, their natural position like running back, wide receiver or defensive back.

This is the deception. There was no natural position for Black kids. Too many times they were pushed into other positions because of White coaches that were totally and completely uninformed. In the ensuing chapters I am going to try to tell the story of Black quarterbacks that stood tall in the pocket, fought through adversity, and truly changed the landscape for the position of quarterback in American Football. Many Black quarterbacks were able to stand up to the athletic establishment in the football world and say "no more.' No more being pushed to the back of the football bus, no more "you have to play running back, wide receiver or defensive back." These Black quarterbacks showed, in a myriad of ways, that they could play quarterback, lead a team, and play championship football. This is truly a story of determination, perseverance and defiance that stood in the face of an archaic system. A system that did not fairly give African American quarterbacks the opportunities they so desperately deserved!

I will also point out a few African American athletes that weren't quarterbacks but played an integral part in the metamorphosis of the Black athlete in American Football.

Marlin Briscoe

The Magician.....too Talented

Marlin Oliver Briscoe born September 10, 1945, died June 27, 2022. His nickname was "The Magician."

Marlin in 1968 was the first Black starting quarterback in professional football leading the AFL's Denver Bronco's.

Briscoe, at the age of nine, would take his football, go out into his front yard, and try to hit a tree. At first he had limited success, but he eventually got better. His quarterback role model was Johnny Unitas, the same as Joe Namath. Quarterbacks from time in memoriam have been throwing at things. Sammy Baugh used to throw at an old tire hanging from a tree.

Joe Namath

In high school his senior year Marlin changed from the quarterback position to running back to help his team win. He knew he could do both positions and do them both very well. Marlin as a running back led his team to a State Championship. After winning the State Championship he and a White teammate went to a local bowling alley to get a sandwich. He was not allowed to eat in the bowling alley because he was Black. They put the high school quarterback's sandwich in a paper bag and made him eat outside. Marlin did not get mad or bitter. His belief was that there were good people in the world even when dreadful things happen. He would let his performance on the field speak for itself as Marlin Briscoe always did. When he tried out for youth football his head coach asked for quarterbacks to go to one area and Marlin was the only African

American to try out for quarterback. His youth coach asked him if he was sure he wouldn't rather be in a different line, like wide receivers or running backs, but Marlin stood tall and said," no, I am a quarterback." As soon as his youth coach saw him throw, he said to young Marlin," you are a quarterback." After a great high school career Marlin did not get college offers to play quarterback.

Briscoe, being a great player out of high school at Omaha South where he became an all-city player, should have received many scholarship offers. Because of his size, 5'9 and slight of weight 155 lbs., and the fact that he only wanted to play quarterback even though he had switched to running back to help his high school team, he was a quarterback. No one wanted this diminutive quarterback except one coach, Al Caniglia from Omaha College, the Mavericks. Coach Caniglia promised Marlin two things; one, he could play quarterback and two, he would get a good college education. Marlin heard enough, he was all in. Briscoe attended Omaha University from 1963 to 1967 and became the starting quarterback. He led his conference in passing and made All First Team in the conference. He broke all kinds of records the following year and led his college team to a championship. It was at this time he also received the nickname "The Magician" because the plays that Marlin made on the field were Houdini-esque. People had never seen a quarterback escape from defensive pressure like Briscoe. He could manufacture plays out of thin air, and consistently make something of nothing. This of course was a precursor to the way the Pro Game is played today. Marlin Briscoe was ahead of the curve. Marlin was having an incredible junior year when he was injured playing pick-up basketball. The injury was so serious he was told he would never play football again. But once again Briscoe was able to overcome. He rehabilitated his neck injury and the doctors told him much to their amazement he was healed and could play football again. Marlin was such a great athlete that the Pittsburg Pirates were interested in him, but Marlin knew that his destiny was on the football field. His senior year he threw for 2,283 yards and 25 touchdowns. Briscoe earned NAIA All American honors.

He played many sports in high school and starred at running back for his team and won. He then attended Omaha University from 1963 to 1967. He left college with a record of 27-11 at the quarterback position and three conference titles, 22 school record completions (55%), 4,935 passing yards, 52 touchdown passes and a total of 6,253 offensive yards. Briscoe was inducted into the College Football Hall of Fame in 2016.

Briscoe was not big at 5'10" and 177 pounds. The Denver Broncos drafted Briscoe in the 14th round in 1968. Denver made Marlin the 357th overall selection in the 1968 Pro football draft. Marlin told Denver if he could not get a tryout as a quarterback, he would return home and become a teacher.

The Dallas Cowboys were also extremely interested in Briscoe. Gil Brandt, the genius personnel manager thought Marlin had tremendous potential as a quarterback. Brandt thought Marlin was the quickest quarterback he had ever seen. New Orleans scout Dave Smith said that Marlin had the best arm of any quarterback in the Pro Draft in 1968. Smith had never seen a right-handed quarterback roll-out left and throw the ball down field 55 yards to the right with pinpoint accuracy. But in 1968 the Broncos called Marlin Brisco and told him that they were going to draft him as a defensive back. Can you imagine how difficult it was for Marlin to hear that! All that he had accomplished as a quarterback, the esoteric skills that he possessed as a passer, runner, leader, and winner, to hear that all you have done at the quarterback position, and it did not seem to count for anything. Always the African American quarterback was looked at in a separate way in the NFL. Looked at as an outstanding athlete that needed to be a wide receiver, defensive back or running back. It was simply wrong on so many levels. Why not bring great athleticism to the quarterback position?

Briscoe was the first starting Black quarterback in the history of professional football in 1968. He started five games in 1968, he threw for 1,589 yards and 14 touchdowns and rushed for 308 yards, three scores and three rushing touchdowns. But the very next season number 15 for the Broncos did not get a chance to compete for the quarterback position. You must ask the very difficult question of why not? The performance numbers were there. Almost Rookie of the Year, then the next season you do not even get a chance to compete for the position. Why would that happen? I remember watching glimpses of Number 15 in the Denver Blue and Red with the Bronco on the helmet making plays, running around and being an improv guy. He made very untraditional plays in a Pro game that was built on traditions. Briscoe was Patrick Mahomes before Patrick Mahomes. With his sensational rookie start at quarterback for the Broncos, the fact that he never got another opportunity to compete for the quarterback job in Denver defies all sports logic. Hank Stram, Head Coach of the Kansas City Chiefs and Super Bowl winner said of Brisco, "He is the most dangerous, scrabbling quarterback that I have seen in nine years in the league. He is like playing against 12 men."

The Bronco's Marlin Brisco's life was full of many ironies. He grew up idolizing Johnny Unitas, number 19 and quarterback of the Baltimore Colts. Certainly, the quarterback type that was remarkable, but also so very representative of conservative, White middle America. The classic "Butch Haircut" and high-top black shoes, truly a touchstone for white working America in the 1960's. And here comes this skinny Black quarterback with a dynamic arm and magical feet that allowed him to escape a charging line that wanted to snap this human toothpick in two. Marlin was different, it is as if he stepped in 1968, into a future transfer machine that wanted people to get a glimpse of what pro football would be like in the year 2023. There is an old saying, "the first one through the wall gets beat up." Marlin Briscoe was the first person through the wall in pro football. Marlin Briscoe was bludgeoned by the system that was set-up in pro football for a White man to play quarterback. Briscoe was traded to the Buffalo Bills in 1969. They already had three established quarterbacks, Jack Kemp (later a congressperson), Dan Darragh, and James Harris (James was African American.) Marlin Briscoe knew that the quarterback room was way too crowded, and he was not going to get the opportunity to play quarterback in Buffalo. Buffalo now asked this extraordinarily talented quarterback to switch to wide receiver. Briscoe did that, as upsetting as that was, and became an all-pro receiver with Buffalo and then later won two Super Bowls with the Miami Dolphins. One of those teams was the 1972 undefeated team, the only one in the history of the NFL.

On first look you might say, so what if Brisco did not get to play quarterback in pro football, he ended up in the College Football Hall of Fame and he made a living in the NFL for nine years and won two Super Bowls. So how was Briscoe Hurt? I would tell you he was wronged significantly by a system in the 1960's that was run by White team owners, White team coaches and a white Football Commissioner. I believe that anytime someone is denied an opportunity with this skill set, it creates a hole, a lack of completeness, a lack of being fulfilled. You know that you have this esoteric talent 98% of the world does not possess and yet because of institutional racism you are denied the fulfillment of your talent. That type of disappointment steals your soul. Life is so ironic most times and such is the case for the first Black quarterback in the history of Pro football. When Marlin Briscoe moved to the Buffalo Bills and switched to wide receiver, he was denied his true destiny in pro football because of a professional

- TOM COLE -

system built to deny opportunity at the quarterback position to athletes that were other than White. But the true irony for Marlon Briscoe was that when he got to Buffalo and was not going to be able to compete at the quarterback position, he switched positions and roomed with James Harris, another Black quarterback. Harris too his credit claimed Brisco helped him so much. Brisco helped Harris to survive at the quarterback position and eventually to become the first African American quarterback to lead a team to an NFL Championship, as he did with the Rams. Even though Briscoe was denied his opportunity he helped another African American reach part of his dream by quarterbacking in the NFL.

Marlin Briscoe retired from the gridiron following the 1976 NFL season. He had 1,697 passing yards, 14 touchdowns, 3,537 receiving yards and 30 receiving touchdowns in his eight-year pro football career from 1969 to 1976. When the Broncos sent rookie Marlin Briscoe in to play quarterback for Denver, people sitting in the seats that day did not understand that they were at that moment looking into the very future of the quarterback position in the NFL. With just a little less than ten minutes to play in the Denver home opener against the Boston Patriots the 14th round draft pick nicknamed "the Magician" threw his first pass, a 22-yard completion to Eric Crabtree. The next drive Briscoe had he took his team 80 yards and made an electric 12-yard touchdown run. That day was a historic day in the NFL. The fans sitting in the stands eating hot dogs and drinking Pepsi might not have truly understood the historical moment that they were in; Marlin "the Magician" became the first Black quarterback to play quarterback in the American Football League. Then one week later Robert Frost Path, that had never been taken before, became the first Black quarterback to start a Pro Game in the modern era of Pro football. That game against the Cincinnati Bengals was earth moving in Pro Football. So, the 1968 rookie season went so very well for the Magician, Marlin Brisco. He passed for 1,589 yards and 14 touchdowns, a team rookie record. He also rushed for 308 yards. How do you have a young skilled athletic run pass quarterback play so very well for you as a rookie and the next year 1969 you trade him to Buffalo. How does that happen? How is that possible? Once Briscoe got to Buffalo his talent had to be the talk of the AFL. His skills were electric. Yet when Marlin got to Buffalo, they were not going to play him at quarterback, he was switched to wide receiver. Can you imagine what had to be going through Briscoe's mind? What did he have to do to be able to play quarterback in Pro football, he certainly had proved his metal. Yet in Buffalo in 1969 he changed positions, caught 32 passes for 532 yards and 5 touchdowns. The next year with Buffalo, Marlin caught 57 passes for 1,036 yards and 8 touchdowns. He was named all AFC and voted to the Pro Bowl. Then after that remarkable year Briscoe was traded to the Miami Dolphins. Briscoe continued to play very well for the Dolphins earning two Super Bowl rings and playing on the famous 17-0 undefeated Miami Team. He then finished his career with the Chargers, Lions and Patriots. When Marlin died at 76 years of age, he carried the banner for all the African American quarterbacks that would follow him. When Briscoe passed Warren Moon said that "he was so very sad" because Briscoe was one of the only Black quarterbacks out there that gave him inspiration that he could become a Black Pro quarterback. Warren Moon sits in the Pro Football Hall of Fame today. I do not think he would be there without Marlin "the Magician" Briscoe. Marlin Briscoe was the originator.

Marlin Briscoe as Robert Frost once said:

"I shall be telling this with a sigh. Somewhere ages and ages hence! Two roads diverged in a wood, and I – I took the one less traveled by, and that has made all the difference."

Marlon Brisco took a different path and helped to break through the institutional racism that existed in the 60's and 70's in pro football in America. American Sports is far better off today because he took this path. The Magician took a different path, and we are all grateful that he did.

MARLIN BRISCOE
15
DENVER BRONCO'S

Marlin Briscoe's time at quarterback in Denver is a lot like a line from a famous Rolling Stones song. "You can't always get what you want but if you try sometimes, you can get what you need!" Marlin should have had more opportunities at quarterback in Denver. It was not fair. But he got what he needed, a career in the NFL and two Super Bowl Rings. Those rings were earned at wide receiver. Given a system that was unbiased, he may have gotten them at his rightful spot at quarterback.

James "Rambling Man" Harris

James "Rambling Man" Harris was a championship quarterback in Los Angeles, he wore number 12. James had two nicknames, one from a name a Baptist minister gave him, Meshach which was shortened to Shack. Rambling Man was a second nickname from a song that was written about James Harris by Sam Spence called "Rambling Man." James, in college at Grambling, won four league titles and was the 1967 MVP of the Orange Blossom Classic. Harris was specifically trained as a prototypical pocket passer by his college coach Eddie Robinson. Shack broke numerous passing records at Grambling.

James was drafted in the eighth round by the American Football League's Buffalo Bills in 1969. He was a rookie with OJ Simpson. The Buffalo Bills made Harris the first Black quarterback to start a season in the history of Pro Football. Marlin Briscoe started in Denver after 5 games but did not start the season. The remarkable irony for James Harris as starting quarterback in Buffalo was on that historic Day the AFL Buffalo Bills quarterback's passes went to none other than Mr. Marlin Briscoe. What a harbinger of things to come. The irony of all ironies. But this was not to be a fantastic Hollywood success story. Three total years in Buffalo, James only started three games, with minimal success and then in 1972 Harris was cut by the Buffalo Bills and picked up by the LA Rams.

In 1973 Harris became an understudy to the Hall of Fame quarterback John Hadl as the Rams put up a 12-2 record and made it back into the playoffs. James Harris, playing in Buffalo and Los Angeles, said that he would not have survived the difficulties of life as a Black quarterback in the NFL without the counseling and advice from his good friend Marlin Briscoe. Briscoe helped Harris to navigate the very rough waters of the NFL for an African American quarterback.

In 1974 in Los Angeles with the Rams, No 12 "the Rambling Man" came to be the starter mid-season and led the Rams to a 7-2 mark. He helped get the Rams into the playoffs. James then led the Rams to their first playoff win in 23 years. James smashed through a pro football ceiling to become the first African American quarterback to start and win a playoff game in the NFL.

In 1974 James Harris was the first Black quarterback named to the Pro Bowl, first Black quarterback to start the Pro Bowl and to be named MVP. Harris remained the starting quarterback in 1975 for the Rams. James led the Rams that year to an impressive 11-2 record, but that year the Rams suffered an opening playoff loss. In 1976 Pat Haden out of USC came to the LA Rams and James "Rambling Man" Harris was traded to the San Diego Chargers where he would stay three seasons as a journeyman. It was a soft parade exit for Harris in San Diego.

The real touchstone question to me looking at Harris' success is how is it that the Rams let him go? His starting record with LA was 21-6. Any Pro Football team today would take that for their starting quarterbacks' three-year record. That is a winning percentage of 77%. How do you let that quarterback go? It does not make any sense. James Harris was big, 6'4, 210 lbs. and very agile, able to move around, very smart, and understood what defenses were trying to do to him. He was a classic drop-back thrower. So, what happened, how could this record setting quarterback be traded to the San Diego Chargers? First you have to look at the Head Coach of the Rams during Harris' time and that was Chuck (Ground Chuck) Knox. Knox was one of those Pro Coaches that believed that a winning formula in Pro Football was to run the ball, play good defense and not turn the ball over. Anyone who ever played quarterback for Knox, I believe, found it a very frustrating experience. John Hadl, Ron Jaworski, James Harris, Pat Haden and Joe Namath, the quarterbacks under him, could never play loose. They were always looking over their shoulders anytime they threw an interception. You cannot play well long term that way at the quarterback position. You have to be able to play through mistakes. During a cold rainy night in Chicago, Joe Namath, starting for Knox and the Rams threw several interceptions and the Rams lost. At the time, the Rams were 3-2 and early in the season. Namath was just learning a new system and new players. The Rams had a good team, Knox just needed to give Namath more time. He benched Joe for the rest of the season and the Rams lost again in the first round of the playoffs. Chuck Knox will never, ever be known as a quarterback friendly Head Coach, he was a quarterback killer. Knox deserved a good amount of credit for giving the first African American quarterback in LA and the Rams a chance, but he should have stayed with Harris just like he should have stayed with Namath. James Harris felt it was always difficult to play for "Gound Chuck" Knox because he was always looking over his shoulder, fearing that he would make a mistake. The fear would become a self-fulfilling prophecy. "Ground Chuck" Knox destroyed quarterbacks with his pedestrian offense and his quick hook for mistakes. James Harris deserved better than being shipped to the graveyard of quarterbacks in the 70's, the San Diego Chargers. Even the great Johnny Unitas went there to die at the quarterback position. James deserved a better fate.

There was so much more to James Harris' career than just his life in Pro Football. Before his incredible iconic career ended with the San Diego Chargers, there were many historical Pro Football foundational markers that quarterback James Harris had accumulated. James Harris made NFL history week one of the 1975 season. When James took the field September 21, 1975, against the Dallas Cowboys in Texas Stadium he became the first Black quarterback to start the season for an NFL team. It did not go to well for Harris that day, it was not a Hollywood movie start. James went 1 for 10 passing for five yards and three interceptions for an 18-7 loss. There were to be many better days. James Harris would also go on to be credited as the first Black quarterback to start in an NFL post season game. James was also the first Black quarterback to lead his team to a division title and to play for a conference championship and the first Black quarterback to lead his conference in passing efficiency. But all this pro success did not come easy. In fact, its origins and beginnings were rooted in speech. When Harris was 16 years old, he sat around a Black and White TV in Monroe Louisiana with his siblings and watched a truly life changing event. It was August 28, 1963, at the Lincoln Memorial in Washington DC. Martin Luther King gave his truly remarkable "I Have a Dream" speech. This prophetic speech sent shock waves through young James Harris. Dr. King's words, *"so even though we face the difficulties of today and tomorrow, I still have a dream. It is a dream deeply rooted in the American Dream. I have a dream that one day this nation will rise up and live out the true meaning of its creed. We hold these truths to be self-evident that all men are created equal"* grabbed James Harris by the front of his high school letter jacket and shook him violently. The football season for James High School team went well, they were undefeated, and they won the championship, and young Harris was the quarterback. Yet before Dr. King's speech James was set to ask his head coach to switch him to a defensive back because he knew as a Black quarterback, he would not get a chance to play Pro Ball at the quarterback position. Black men were precluded from playing that position because old white coaches and old white owners did not believe that a Black quarterback would be able to handle the playbook and that the majority of white football players on the team would not follow a Black quarterback leader. These views were so incredibly ignorant it is exceedingly difficult to understand how people could have adopted them. But this earth-shaking speech by Dri King spoke directly to James Harris, it went directly to his soul, it struck his heart, mind, and body. This speech by Dr. King told James he was not going to change his position. He was intelligent, he was a leader, he was gifted and No 12 was born to play quarterback in the NFL. Dr. King with his life-changing words showed a very young 16-year-old what his true path could be.

James made a great football decision to attend Grambling State to play under the Legendary Coach Eddie Robinson from 1965 to 1968. Coach Robinson trained James Harris to be a classic pocket passing quarterback. His coach already had his eye on the Pro Game for James as a starting quarterback in the NFL. James Harris has been inducted into the Southwestern Athletic Conference Hall of Fame, the Louisiana Sports Hall of Fame, and the Black College Football Hall of Fame. James helped to tutor Doug Williams the first American quarterback to start and win the Super Bowl. James also kicked down another door of racial opposition in the NFL. He served as the Baltimore Ravens Director of Pro Personnel from 1997 to 2003. During his tenure the Ravens made it to the Super Bowl and won it in Super Bowl XXXV. He also was Vice President of Player Personnel for the Jacksonville Jaguars. James opened other doors in professional football for Black Athletes not just at the quarterback position but for front office jobs in the NFL.

James Harris played in the NFL from 1969 to 1979. During his career he played with the Buffalo Bills, Los Angeles Rams, and the San

Diego Chargers. James Harris threw for 8,136 yards in his NFL career at quarterback. He also threw 45 touchdowns and had 59 interceptions. James also ran for 367 yards in 121 attempts with 10 rushing touchdowns.

To me when I think of number 12 James Harris at quarterback, I think of him as an LA Ram. Big number 12 in the Ram helmet with the blue and gold colors and that gigantic face mask he used to wear. Harris in the pocket stood tall like a giant oak tree, fearless, steady, never worrying about the pass rush around him. He displayed courage every time he dropped back looking downfield trying to find a Ram receiver running free in the secondary. Number 12 James Harris was always a man of great intelligence, character, toughness, and the desire to help fulfill Dr. King's message helping to create opportunities for other Black quarterbacks. He was iconic, a touchstone quarterback in the NFL advancing opportunities for other African American quarterbacks in football. James proved what Dr. King said on August 28, 1963, that it is not the color of your skin but the content of your character. James Harris proved that every day in the NFL with skill, toughness, leadership, desire and game intelligence. James Harris the "Ramblin Man" at quarterback was able to overcome the myopic view that the NFL had in his time, that a Black QB could not lead a majority White team, so others that came after James could be free to have a fair chance to succeed.

The early days of the NFL 1950's, 1960's, 1970's and into the 1980's, the NFL had the earmarking of a caste system. Where the White owners and White coaches had their quota of Black players on their team and truly few Black quarterbacks. That was by design. In 1988 when Doug (I can throw it deep on anyone) Williams became the first quarterback to start and win a Super Bowl, one would think this archaic caste system; the athletic plantation system of particular designs to limit and control Black participation in the NFL especially at the quarterback position would be broken into smithereens. But it was not so. Racist views do not go away easily. It took, unbelievably another 26 years after Doug Williams was the first Black QB to win a Super Bowl to have Russell Wilson come along, another standout African American quarterback that won a super bowl with Seattle in 2014. Things in the NFL were getting better as far as looking through the lens of race at the quarterback position, but the NFL still had some distance to travel. But certainly James Harris, Big Number 12 for the LA Rams helped to make that road for other Black Quarterbacks just a little easier.

JAMES HARRIS

12

LOS ANGELES RAMS

James Shack Harris' song is Rambling Man ......the lyrics by the Allman Brothers. *"So Lord I was born a rambling man, trying to make a living doing the best I can and when its time for leavin I hope you understand that I was born a rambling man..."*

Chuck Ealey
"Mr. Ohhh's and Ahh's"

Chuck Ealey, is a recent inductee into the College Football Hall of Fame. Chuck Ealey was so very esoteric as a quarterback, no one compared to him as a player and a man.

In high school, in Portsmouth, Ohio Chuck played quarterback and never lost a game. Chuck Ealey attended high school in Portsmouth at Notre Dame High School. What Chuck did there was so unusual in football, especially at the quarterback position. He NEVER lost a game. If you have ever tried to play the quarterback position, you would truly understand what an amazing accomplishment that was. As a senior at Notre Dame High School and never losing a game you would assume that Ealey, with that kind of incredible record, would be widely recruited by colleges everywhere. This was not the case, why not? Chuck was 5'11" young Black man who played the game differently in the 1960's. He threw from the pocket, but he also moved around and scrambled and improvised. He played the game differently. He was different and he was an African American quarterback in the 1960's. In college there were very few. To his credit Bo Schembechler, then at Miami of Ohio as the head football coach, tried to recruit Ealey but, with a "BUT." Coach Bo later became the immortal Michigan Head Football Coach, told Chuck that he would give him a scholarship but and there was always the, "but" Chuck would need to change positions to running back, wide receiver or defensive back. Can you imagine how much this had to hurt Ealey? He proved his metal at quarterback in Portsmouth by never losing a game. But that is where Ealey's story takes a remarkably interesting turn. Frank Lauterbur from the University of Toledo started recruiting Chuck Ealey, but he came in late. Frank was the outstanding head football coach at the University of Toledo. He had missed Chuck's football season but sent one of his coaches down to Portsmouth to watch Ealey play basketball. This particular game that the UT football scout saw Chuck scored 30 plus points and made the last second shot to win the game for his team. Lauterbur's scout came back and raved about Ealey and what a great athlete he was, so Coach Lauterbur summoned Chuck to the University of Toledo campus and then offered him a scholarship. But an awfully familiar conversation then happened to Mr. Ealey. Coach Lauterbur said he would offer Ealey a scholarship, but he would have to change positions to running back, wide-out, or defensive back. Chuck looked at Coach Lauterbur and said with true conviction, character, and strength, "no coach, I am a quarterback not a running back, wideout or defensive back. Ealey knew who he was and what he could do if given the opportunity. Coach Lauterbur paused a minute, not often does a young man turn down a scholarship, but it gave the coach a pause. This young man believes in himself and his ability to play the quarterback position. The coach right there, on the spot said that young Ealey would get the opportunity to compete for the quarterback position and as is often said, "the rest is history," great college football history. Chuck Ealey then went on at the University of Toledo to quarterback 35 straight victories, never losing a game and three Tangerine Bowl victories. So, Chuck Ealey, "Mr. Ohhs and Ahhhs" proceeded to make spectacular plays on the football field that people in the stands could not believe. They could not even trust their own eyes, because No. 16 often fooled them by making impossible plays. Ealey was recruited by two of the greatest all-time football coaches in the history of college football. Frank Lauterbur and Bo Schembechler, both extremely powerful men at their universities and when they both told Chuck that he would have to change positions and he would not be playing quarterback Chuck believed so strongly in himself and his abilities that he said no; and this changed the landscape of college and pro football forever.

What made Chuck Ealey so remarkable? It was a myriad of elements. I had the opportunity to speak to several of his football teammates. One such teammate was Mike Archambeau, a former Bowsher High School football star and member of the University of Toledo 35-0 football team and a successful physical therapist in Toledo, Ohio. I asked Mike, an incredibly astute gentleman, what made Chuck different at quarterback, being able to lead a team of Black and White players during a time of tremendous racial tension in our country? Mike paused for a moment, then reflectively said, "Chuck never saw color, he treated every team member with respect. He made every team member feel important. It was never about Chuck." He went on to say, "Chuck had the ability to meet the moment, rise up and make plays at crucial times. He was a quarterback that did not have the strongest arm, was not the fastest runner but if you put him in a clutch situation, he always made the play. When you do that enough in football and time after time lead your team to victories when it looked very bleak, you develop at the quarterback position a sense of invincibility that you can't lose and people in that huddle play harder for you". That is truly the intangible that Number 16 possessed in the University of Toledo huddle, that feeling that the "Rockets" can't lose because they had Number 16 in the huddle. And they did not lose for 35 straight games.

Chuck Ealey, a recent inductee into the college football Hall of Fame, had a high school, college and Pro career that would make a classic Disney movie. Chuck Ealey was a Black man that played the game differently in the 1960's and 70's as a quarterback. He threw very accurately from the pocket but when trouble happened, he had a unique ability to move around, to scramble to improvise to make a play out of nothing and drive defenses crazy. Ealey played the game differently.

Chuck and his remarkable University of Toledo Rockets, who did the almost impossible, winning 35 regular season games in a row, almost did not happen early in the streak. The incredibly young University of Toledo streak was at four in a row with no thoughts of thirty-five. Ealey and his Rockets were living the old sports cliche one game at a time. They were playing their hated rival in the sports sense, Bowling Green State University. It was October 11, 1969. The Rockets trailed the stalwart Bowling Green Falcons 26-24 with 49 seconds on the clock. Ealey, "Mr. Calm, just another day at the office" walked into the Toledo huddle and looked at all his tired, beat-up guys in their eyes and just said, "Let's go to work!" Chuck ran 7 plays in 47 seconds and got his very tired Rockets to the Bowling Green 21-yard line with 2 seconds remaining. If you have ever attended or played football at Bowling Green University, you understand the unbelievable wind tunnel that exists on the Bowling Green Field. The wind was howling in the face of the Rockets when their kicker, Ken Crots, lined up to try a 21-yard field goal into this gale force wind. Folklore has it that Chuck put his arms up on the sideline to calm the wind, folklore like Paul Bunyan or Davey Crocket. But still old timers that were in the stands that fateful day will swear on everything that is sacred to them that just as Ken Crots hit the ball and it headed toward the goal line the wind stopped, it stopped, it really did, and the kick went through and the very young Rocket winning streak continues.

There was another game in the streak to 35 for the University of Toledo and Ealey that was very dicey. The Rockets, late in a game in 1969, were tied with Villanova 7-7 with 29 seconds to play. The Rockets and Ealey had the ball at their 29-yard line. Again, Mr. Calm told his wide receiver Glenn Smith to run a go pattern on the sideline and to run as far and as fast as he could. Ealey then told his tired UT linemen to block as long as they could, it would take Glenn a while to get that far down field; and Chuck said he would move around a little if he had to. Chuck did just that, bought time by "moving around" just a little and then in the dimly lit Glass Bowl Ealey unleashed a 57-yard bomb that Smith caught and was tossed out of bounds. In came the field goal kicker for Toledo with a couple of seconds on the clock and kicks the field goal and the unbeaten streak for Toledo continued. It is truly incomprehensible that a quarterback that won 35 straight football games with his teammates at the University of Toledo would not get a chance to play quarterback in the NFL. But that was Ealey's situation. How can a young man who played that position so very well, better than anyone who has ever played in college not get drafted in the NFL, and only voted 11th in the Heisman Trophy. That trophy was supposed to epitomize someone that meant the most to his team. Chuck proved how much he meant to his Toledo Teammates. There were inquiries about Chuck from the NFL but with one caveat, that he has heard many times before, would you change positions. Changing positions after 35 straight college wins and three bowl victories. Once again Chuck stood his ground. He did not back down. He went to Canada to play professional football and those of you who know the remarkable Chuck Ealey story, his first year in Canada he won the Grey Cup. The Canadian equivalent of the Super Bowl. On top of that if you can imagine this extraordinary talent, Chuck Ealey never became bitter about the NFL or the College Football Hall of Fame. He was disappointed it took him 50 years to get into the College Hall of Fame, but all Chuck did was continue to succeed in business after football in Canada. He inspired people to stick to their goals, beliefs, and principles. Chuck is a devoted family man and a trusted and valued leader in his Canadian hometown and in Toledo Ohio with his "Undefeated Spirit Organization", that helps students and adults alike reach their dreams. He is an incredible community mentor.

Chuck's college career was a Hollywood movie. He and his teammates were undefeated for three years, including winning three bowl games. He passed for 5000 yards and 42 touchdowns. He ran for 900 yards and 12 touchdowns. Then the NFL told him he had to switch positions, or nobody would draft him. Chuck then moved onto the Canadian football League. His First year in the CFL as a rookie he threw for 22 touchdowns and 2500 yards and led the Hamilton Tiger Cats to win the Grey Cup. He also won the MVP of the game.

Chuck Ealey No. 16 for the University of Toledo Rockets really has been an MVP his entire life. He is an MVP with people. He helps people attain goals. Chuck opens eyes to possibilities, making people understand something Chuck has known his entire life, taught to him by his remarkable Mom, "together we are better."

CHUCK EALEY
16
CANADIAN LEAGUE

- TOM COLE -

Chuck's song......Marvin Gay's *What's Going On*. How could a man, a quarterback with 35 wins in a row, not get a shot in the NFL and have to wait 50 years to get into the College Hall of Fame? *"What's going on, picket lines and picket signs. Don't punish me with brutality, talk to me, so you can see, oh, what's going on, what's going on, what's going on".* Chuck Ealey in the late 60's and early 70's could see what was going on in our racially turbulent times. Every time he stepped into the huddle or out into the street, he made the world a better place.

Joe Gilliam Jr.
Jefferson Street Joe

Joe Gilliam spent four seasons with the Pittsburg Steelers. Joe was tall and very thin. He had a whippet like release passing motion. Joe was such a standout at quarterback he beat out the Bonde Bomber himself, Hall of Fame quarterback Terry Bradshaw. To Terry's credit he openly admitted that Jefferson Street (Jefferson Street was the street in front of his college) beat him out of the position. Joe Gilliam Jr. was a Black Joe Namath, incredibly quick feet dropping back to throw, and he could back pedal like Joe Willie. And Joe's arm was like Namath, remarkably quick action on the football.

You could see Joe Jr's talent; it was eye popping. It was obvious, and his Pittsburg Steelers teammates knew it, as did Bradshaw. Joe Gilliam's story is all about unfulfilled potential. In high school he was a multiple sport athlete at Peal High School. Joe Jr's father was a defensive coordinator of Tennessee State. Joe Jr. hung around the program as a ball boy and then later attended Tennessee State to play quarterback and did he ever play quarterback, he was remarkable. In 1970 he led Tennessee State to 10-0 and a win in the Grantland Rice Bowl. His team was named the "Black College National Champions. His junior year in college in the books his senior year was more of the same. Joe was named All American.

Then he was drafted by the Pittsburg Steelers in 1972, the 273rd pick overall. Gilliam's first start in Pro Football was a disaster in 1973 against the Dolphins. He threw seven passes all incomplete and three picked off. In 1974 Joe Gilliam won the starting quarterback job over Terry Bradshaw. He was the first African American quarterback to start a Pro Game at quarterback since the 1970 AFL-NFL merger. In six games he was 4-1-1 as the Steelers quarterback but ended up getting benched.

Joe had a good starting record but was benched according to Chuck Noll, the Pittsburg Steelers Head Coach, because he threw the ball too much. Noll was a very conservative ground-oriented coach. Noll also thought Gilliam was not attentive in meetings and focused in practice. Gilliam thought his demotion was racially motivated, most of the Pittsburg Players did not. But that being said a starting quarterback losing his position with a 4-1-1 record is very unusual. But as a former lifelong football coach and quarterback myself what you did in practice and how you focused in meetings is particularly important. Obviously, Noll felt Joe Gilliam was not doing all that he should do and made the switch back to Terry Bradshaw at the starting Steeler quarterback.

When Gilliam lost his starting position at quarterback with the Pittsburg Steelers, he then went into a downward spiral that he could not turn around. Joe Gilliam for the rest of his life dealt with addiction. He also played for a myriad of semi-pro teams across the country. Joe fought his entire life trying to recapture the glory days of being the first starting Black quarterback in the History of the Pittsburg Steelers and making the cover of Sports Illustrated. Gilliam was like a virtuoso violin player, he had this remarkable skill set, tremendous arm, great release, and courage in the pocket with exceptional feet and quickness to back pedal in the pocket. It must be exceedingly difficult to possess this esoteric skill from the quarterback position and yet not be able to harness his addiction problems. Unfulfilled talent must tear at someone's soul, not being able to reach your full potential, knowing that you can do something better than most people, yet you cannot reach your rightful place and stature in pro football because you cannot harness and control your addiction issues. If you have ever been involved with someone with addiction problems, you understand it really has nothing to do with discipline. It is a much more complex issue than just "saying no." It is an illness, a disease, no different than cancer and if untreated will eventually kill you. And that is exactly what happened to Joe Gilliam Jr. After getting three years sober, he slipped as unfortunately happens many times to addicts and Joe passed away from an overdose. Jefferson Street Joe Gilliam was an enigma, incredibly talented and full of unfulfilled promise.

Number 17 "Jefferson Street" Joe Gilliam was a super nova flashing across the Pittsburg skyline in Three Rivers Stadium. That burned brightly but died out way to quickly.

JOE GILLIAM JR.

17

PITTSBURG STEELERS

Joe's song....The Temptations *Ball of Confusion*. *"People moving out, People moving in, Why, because of the color of their skin. Run, run, run but you can't hide"*

Doug Williams
The Black Don Quixote

Doug Williams attended Chaneyville High School in Louisiana. He was originally a linebacker then switched to quarterback. After High School Williams was recruited by Grambling State. He received his degree in 1977. Then he became the First African American quarterback to be drafted in the first round with the Tampa Bay Buccaneers. During his five years at Tampa Bay, he took the Bucks to the play-offs three times.

Doug Williams was never truly appreciated in Tampa. He had one of the strongest arms in the history of the NFL. He used to overthrow receivers often, not Doug's fault, receivers many times did not run through the routes. They were not used to running deep routes with a quarterback that had such a remarkable arm. The ongoing joke in Tampa during Doug's quarterbacking was the only person that he could not overthrow was the Ayatollah. This was unfair to Williams who had such a gifted arm the receivers needed to adjust to him. In 1987 he was traded to the Washington Redskins as a backup to Jay Schroeder. Schroeder was inconsistent, got benched and Doug became the starting quarterback and took the Washington Redskins to Super Bowl XXII. The Redskin receiverS had little trouble tracking Doug's long passes and his offensive Coach Joe Gibbs brilliant offense. The offense was a perfect fit for Doug early on in Super Bowl XXII. Doug hurt his knee from a sack and limped off the field and the millions on television and the sold-out crowd thought that was the end of Williams that day. But Doug had work done on his knee and limped back into the game. What he did with a tremendous display of courage in Super Bowl XXII was throw for 340 yards and four touchdowns and was named MVP. Williams in Super Bowl XXII displayed all the toughness and determination and passing that was more than enough to defeat the Denver Broncos 42-10. Doug was always criticized in his career for overthrowing receivers as stated earlier. He had such a powerful arm his receivers in his early pro days did not understand how powerful his deep arm was. The Washington Redskins figured his arm strength out. Williams had a career 49% completion rate and people used this against him. The reason his completion rate was lower is because often he threw the ball deep. Joe Namath had the same pro completion rate as Doug Williams because he always threw the ball deep. Namath was criticized like Doug Williams for a lower completion rate. Many critics of the game just do not understand that if you consistently throw the ball deep you are going to have a lower completion percentage. Doug Williams became the first African American quarterback to start in a Super Bowl, win and become MVP. Doug totally and completely destroyed the long-held belief by White owners and White coaches that a Black quarterback could lead his team to a Super Bowl victory.

It is so ironic and poignant that when Doug Williams heard for the first time ever two Black quarterbacks would be starting Super Bowl LVII, he got emotional. These were tears, tears of progress and tears of accomplishment. Doug knew that many Black quarterbacks that came after him stood tall on his shoulders. Doug Williams smashed that ceiling, he obliterated it. Forever more there would never be the quiet whispers in corners about if you could win with a Black quarterback. Doug William was a Black Don Quixote, charging at NFL windmills until he slayed his dragon, and he did!

DOUG WILLIAMS

17

TAMPA BAY WASHINGTON

Doug's song.... ***"If We Can Dream"*** *by Elvis Presley. There must be lights burning brighter somewhere, got to be birds flying higher in a sky more Blue, if I can dream of a better land where all my brothers walk hand in hand, tell me why, oh why, oh why can't my dream come true.*

- TOM COLE -

The Duke

There were many Black quarterbacks that pushed into the caste system of professional football and college football for that matter. But there were other African American position players that helped to change the face of pro football, not just quarterbacks.

First to my mind is the extraordinary story of Duke Slater at Iowa, Duke was three time all Big Ten tackle. He led the Hawkeyes to an undefeated season. He also helped to lead his Iowa team to a victory over Knute Rockne's Notre Dame team which had won 20 games in a row.

Duke played for the pro team the Rock Island Independents from 1922 to 1925. He would finish his Pro career with the Chicago Cardinals from 1926 to 1931. Slater played for ten years in pro football. Duke has the longest tenured playing time of any Black player in the 1920's and 1930's. Slater was named All NFL four times in 1923,1925,1926 and 1929. Yet Duke was never named to the NFL All Decade Team. How can that happen? There is no other way to explain it but blind institutional racism in the NFL. It must be so difficult to know that you deserve something, yet you are denied it because of prejudice. It has to eat at your soul, has to leave a whole in your heart making someone feel less than others. But this unfortunate treatment drove Duke Slater even harder to achieve, drove him to greatness. When Duke retired from Pro football, he graduated from law school in 1928 and he became an assistant district attorney.

Duke was elected Judge in 1948, only the second Black Judge in the history of Chicago at that time. Then in 1960 Duke Slater became the first Black Judge to serve on the Superior Court of Chicago. Duke Slater overcame football bias in the Pro's to accomplish greatness on the field and in the courtroom. Eventually Duke was named to the College football Hall of Fame and in 2020 Duke was finally inducted into the Pro Football Hall of Fame posthumously, ninety years after Duke had played. George Halas called Duke a defensive line on his own.

As egregious as this sounds, George Preston Marshall, owner of the Washington Redskins, steered the NFL into a twelve-year ban on Black athletes playing in the National Football League. From 1934 to 1946 NFL owners came together and banned Black players from playing in the National Football League. How could that happen??? Yet bias and prejudice still exists today and in society and in the NFL. There are so few Black owners and very few Black head coaches in a league that is comprised of almost 53% of their players being African American. How is that possible in 2024? That can be easily explained by the acronym OWO (Old White Owners) in the NFL.

The Duke Slater story is certainly not unique, unfortunately, yet Number 16 was a man who we can all look to as a role model. When he played football at Clinton High School in Iowa, the school could only afford to offer a player shoes or a helmet. The Duke wearing size fourteen shoes decided on the football shoes and played in high school without a helmet and played most of his college career without a helmet. So, whenever you are facing difficult problems in your professional life or your personal life remember the Duke, Number 16, he climbed that mountain, nothing could stop him. Duke Slater could not be denied, he made his opportunities, his efforts, talent, grace, and intellect demanded respect. The Duke is a great

American success story that truly defied the odds and inspired so many others.

DUKE SLATER
16
"THE DUKE"

Duke's song...... ***"I Won't Back Down"*** *by Tom Petty ....Well, I won'tback down, no I won't back down. You could stand me up at the gates of Hell, but I won't back down. No, I'll stand my ground, won't be turned around and I'll keep this world from draggin me down. Gonna stand my ground and I won't back down.*

Another non-quarterback position that helped to destroy the caste system in Pro Football for African American players was Kenny Washington. Kenny played his college football and baseball for UCLA and the most well-known professional football team that he played for was the Los Angeles Rams. Kenny was a remarkable athlete playing both football and baseball at UCLA. Kenny Washington played at UCLA the same time that Jackie Robinson did. There were many professional scouts that believed that Kenny Washington was a better baseball prospect than Jackie Robinson, that is how outstanding Kenny was! But football was his true sport. As a young boy he had a bicycle accident and broke both of his knees, which always caused him problems during his football career; having five knee operations and at times wearing a bulky steel brace to be able to play but play he did. Kenny played half back in the Wing-T which meant he was a runner and a passer. Kenny Washington was the first African American player to sign a pro contract after the NFL boycott for Black Players. During WWII Washington signed up for military service, much like Joe Namath, his knees were so damaged from football he could only serve in a ceremonial fashion. He also became a member of the Los Angeles Police Department.

Kenny Washington's real contribution came on the football field. He was admired throughout the Los Angeles Community. He was so revered at his last game in the Los Angeles Coliseum, he received a car, television, and a standing ovation for a prolonged period.

Bob Snyder, Head Coach of the Rams in 1947, coaching Kenny Washington, said, "if Washington had been allowed to play in the NFL in his prime, he would have been the best there ever was, like Robert Redford in the *The Natural."* Kenny Washington was a quasi-quarterback being that he played half back in the single wing and had to throw and run. A lot of the shotgun offenses that are run today have principles from the old T-Formation. As Coach Snyder said, Kenny Washington would have been the best there was, better than Jim Thorpe and Bronko Nagurski. Bob Snyder, who was a personal friend that I had many football conversations with was not a man that was prone to hyperbole. Bob Synder was a football genius, inventor of the T-Formation and for him to say Kenny Washington was that good, you can take that to the bank.

Postscript to Kenny Washington, he still today owns the longest run from the line of scrimmage in the history of the LA Rams, 92 yards. Washington was so revered and admired in the LA Community that the taxpayers, Black citizens and White citizens, put so much pressure on the owners of the LA Colosseum that they said in mass that if the LA Rams did not sign Kenny Washington to a Pro Contract, the people of Los Angeles would refuse to support with tax funds and personal funds, events at the Los Angeles Colosseum. Ownership buckled and Kenny was signed and the rest as they say is history, for the incredible number 13 who was instrumental in busting the NFL color barrier.

KENNY WASHINGTON
13
LOS ANGELES RAMS

*Kenny Washington's song to me would be....**Hold On I'm Coming** by Sam & Dave...."'Don't you ever be sad, lean on me when times are bad. When the day comes and you're down in a river of trouble and about to drown, just hold on I'm comin, hold on I'm comin"*

Every African American quarterback that played in the NFL helped to break down those walls so others could advance. The starting point should be at the beginning of this chronological list of Black quarterbacks that played in the NFL.

Other Gifted African American Quarterbacks Like Fritz Pollard And Warren Moon And Many More

Fritz Pollard was the first Black quarterback in the history of the NFL when he played for the Hammond Pros in 1923. He also became the first All American quarterback in college and the first African American quarterback to appear in the Rose Bowl. Fritz had to fight racism his entire career, from fans and even his own teammates. Pollard would sometimes have to enter the field from a separate gate to be safe from the attack of fans. Some fans chanted "kill him" and threw bottles and bricks at him. But Fritz persevered and after Pro Football he started the first Black newspaper called *"The New York Independent."* And, finally, justly, and correctly Fritz Pollard was inducted into the Pro Football Hall of Fame in 2005.

Warren Moon of the Houston Oilers was one of the best passers ever in Pro Football. Warren could not get what he originally wanted from the NFL which was a real shot to quarterback a team. He had to go to Canada where he found incredible success and then come back to the NFL where he eventually became a Hall of Famer.

Patrick Mahomes is the face of Pro Football and the quarterback position. He makes plays on the field that are incredible. Patrick Mahomes is the new prototype at quarterback in the NFL. He can beat you from the pocket or on a scramble or in a made-up improvised play in the dirt.

Randall Cunningham was one of the most athletic quarterbacks to ever step onto an NFL Field. He was big, strong, fast, and able to recognize defenses very well and make all the plays.

Donovan McNabb was one of the first true Black quarterbacks that was a Pro Pocket Passer. He would beat you throwing from the pocket. Donovan was a remarkable leader who understood the passing game very well.

Lamarr Jackson is a unique combination of speed and play making ability combined with exceptionally good passing skills.

Steve McNair had one of the best passing arms in the history of the NFL. He was one of the toughest quarterbacks. He stood in the pocket and took a ton of punishment. He was a warrior, a true downhill thrower.

Michael Vick has the fastest foot speed at the quarterback position in the history of the NFL. Bad decisions in his personal life took his talent away.

Russell Wilson regardless of his limited size was able to find windows in the pocket and throw play action and half rolls to be an effective all Pro Quarterback.

Cam Newton is one of the biggest and strongest quarterbacks to ever play professional football. Cam played with total disregard for his physical health. He threw the ball and his body around with no fear.

A Coach that Broke the Black Ceiling

The Michigan State Head Football Coach in the 1960's was the great Duffy Daugherty. Duffy was one of those true difference makers for African American athletes playing college football, and for getting Black athletes to the NFL and helping them to receive a college education. Daugherty assembled in 1966 the first fully integrated football roster, with twenty Black players. One of the twenty Black players was Jimmy Raye quarterback for Michigan State. In 1966 the game of the century was played between two undefeated teams, Notre Dame, and Michigan State. Americans watched, 33 million viewers, for the first time a team that had starting Black players at many positions. It was a remarkable game that ended in a 10-10 tie.

The Michigan State quarterback came from the segregated south to Michigan. He was told by Coach Duffy Daugherty that he would be able to play quarterback and would not be switchd to wide receiver or defensive back. Raye was an incredible quarterback for Michigan State. He led them to a National Championship and a Big Ten Title. Yet Raye went to high school in the South and when he came to Michigan State, he traveled by train 36 hours (about 1 and a half days). His mother packed Jimmy lunch in a shoebox for the incredibly long train ride. It consisted of chicken and baloney sandwiches. It smelled so good to Jimmy Raye that he could not wait and ate the entire lunch box in the first few hours. Raye could not go to the food club car on the train until the train had crossed the Mason Dixon Line, more indignities on top of other indignities for African American Football players in the 60's in America. Coach Duffy Daugherty was a true difference maker. He recognized that football as a game, helped to teach social mores, lessons in life. Duffy Daugherty made sure his players understood civil rights fairness and equality. Duffy Daugherty was a true teacher.

Deal Me In

Sometimes the integration of sports or the integration of life has been moved forward faster by individual deeds like in the momentous moment when Rosa Parks decided she would not move to the back of the bus on December 1, 1955. In Sport it was a Major League All-Star game, and a good part of America was still segregated. Stan Musial from the St. Louis Cardinals was an immense star in the National League of Professional Baseball. He walked into the locker room hours before the All-Star Game and what Stan saw when he came into the locker room of the All-Stars was the White All-Star players sitting on one side and the Black All-Star players were on the other side of the locker room playing cards, Black super stars Willie Mays, Hank Aaron. Stan the Man did not hesitate, he went directly to the Black players and just said, "deal me in." Musial sat and played cards with his Black All-Star teammates. That surely caught the attention of White baseball stars. This simple act by "Stan the Man" Musial, who understood what it meant to be a teammate changed some minds and actions of Major League Baseball players.

The Cafeteria

When Joe Namath was drafted by the New York Jets and was paid more money than any quarterback had ever been paid. He found the Jets had a practice he did not understand or agree with. When the Jets went to lunch break during training camp in August of 1965, he was shocked to see that the cafeteria was divided in two, there were Black players eating together then on another side White players eating lunch together. This was not done by management, the players did it themselves. Namath grew up in integrated neighborhoods in Beaver Falls, Pennsylvania. His best pals in school were Black. So, when Namath walked into the Jet's cafeteria for lunch with his teammates, he took his tray of food and went right over to the Black table and sat down and ate his lunch. That gesture changed a lot of things on the New York Jets Football team who would in four short years go on to win Super Bowl III in 1969. Namath's gesture changed racial attitudes on the Jets team just like Musial helped to open eyes in baseball for fairer treatment for minority players.

Sometimes it Takes a Group

Sometimes it takes a group to make a difference and to stand up and not compromise their values. January 9, 1965 was the AFL All-Star Game in New Orleans. The segregation was so bad at that time the Black AFL Football All-Stars could not get a cab from the airport to their hotel. Blacks were not allowed to ride in a cab with a White cab driver. Once the players found cabs with Black drivers they eventually got to the hotel. Then the players tried to go down to Burbon Street to try the world-famous food. It was made noticeably clear that they were not welcome. They could not hang their coats up next to White people's coats. Some of the Black players had a gun put in their faces telling them if they tried to come into a nightclub they would be shot. The players eventually made it back to their hotels and had had enough. They held a meeting and decided they would not play the game. They all returned home, the game was canceled and moved later to Houston.

Because the Black Players stood up for themselves some changes were starting to happen for the betterment of New Orleans. About five years later the City of New Orleans was awarded an NFL franchise, the Saints.

Change is difficult but as a group standing up to discrimination in this horrible situation, they made a difference. Their dramatic statement improved the City of New Orleans and the manner in which they dealt with race. Football can be a great metaphor for life and a valuable tool to teach meaningful life lessons.

Every Starting African American Quarterback in Pro Football Who are your favorites

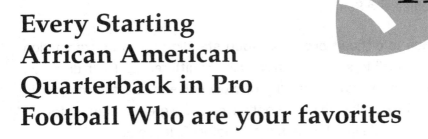

Fritz Pollard 1920 Akron Pros

Joe Lillard 1932 Chicago

George Taliaferro 1950 New York Yanks

Willie Thrower (Great name for a quarterback) 1953 Chicago Bears

Charlie Brackins 1955 Green Bay Packers

Sandy Stephens 1962 Cleveland Browns

Dave Lewis 1967 New York Giants

Marlin Briscoe 1968 Denver Broncos

Eldridge Dickey 1968 Oakland Raiders

James Harris 1969 Buffalo Bills

Karl Douglas 1971 Baltimore Colts

Joe Gilliam 1972 Pittsburg Steelers

Dave Mays 1976 Cleveland Browns

J.J. Jones 1975 New York Jets

Parnell Dickinson 1976 Tampa Bay Buccaneers

John Walton 1976 Philadelphia Eagles

Vince Evans 1977 Chicago Bears

Doug Williams 1978 Tampa Bay Buccaneers

Nickie Hall 1981 Green Bay Packers

Warren Moon 1984 Houston Oilers

Brian Ransom 1983 Houston Oilers

Randall Cunningham 1985 Philadelphia Eagles

Reggie Collier 1986 Dallas Cowboys

Willie Totten 1987 Buffalo Bills

Bernard Quarles 1987 LA Rams

Willie Gillus 1987 Green Bay Packers

Mark Stevens 1987 San Francisco 49ers

Ed Blount 1987 San Francisco 49ers

Kevin Robinson 1987 Washington Redskins

Ricky Turner 1988 Indianapolis Colts

Don McPherson 1988 Philadelphia Eagles

Rodney Peete 1989 Detroit Lions

Steve Taylor 1989 Indianapolis Colts

Terrence Jones 1989 San Diego Chargers

Andre Ware 1990 Detroit Lions

Clemente Gordon 1990 Cleveland Browns

Major Harris 1990 L.A. Rams

Reggie Slack 1990 Houston Oilers

Shawn Moore 1991 Denver Broncos

Jeff Blake 1992 New York Jets

Keithen McCant 1992 Cleveland Browns

Jay Walker 1994 New England

Steve McNair 1995 Houston Oilers

Kordell Stewart 1995 Pittsburgh Steelers

Tony Banks 1996 St. Louis Rams

Ray Lucas 1996 New England Patriots

Wally Richardson 1997 Baltimore Ravens

Charlie Batch 1998 Detroit Lions

Donavan McNabb 1999 Philadelphia Eagles

Akili Smith 1999 Cincinnati Bengals

Daunte Culpepper 2000 Minnesota Vikings

Aaron Brooks 1999 Green Bay Packers

Michael Bishop 1999 New England Patriots

Anthony Wright 1999 Pittsburgh Steelers

Shawn King 1999 Tampa Bay Buccaneers

Dameyune Craig 2000 Carolina Panthers

Spergon Wynn 2000 Cleveland Browns

Tee Martin 2000 Pittsburgh Steelers

Joe Hamilton 2000 Tampa Bay Buccaneers

Jarious Jackson 2000 Denver Broncos

Henry Burris 2001 Green Bay Packers

Tory Woodbury 2001 New York Jets

Quincy Carter 2001 Dallas Cowboys

Michael Vick 2001 Atlanta Falcons

Rohan Davey 2002 New England Patriots

David Garrard 2002 Jacksonville Jaguars

Brian Leftwich 2003 Jacksonville Jaguars

Seneca Wallace 2006 Seattle Seahawks

Quinn Gray 2004 Jacksonville Jaguars

Cleo Lemon 2006 San Diego Chargers

Jason Campbell 2005 Washington Red Skins

Reggie McNeal 2006 Cincinnati Bengals

Marcus Vick 2006 Miami Dolphins

Vince Young 2006 Tennessee Titans

Tarvaris Jackson 2006 Minnesota Vikings

Brad Smith 2006 New York Jets

JaMarcus Russell 2007 Oakland Raiders

Troy Smith 2007 Baltimore Ravens

Dennis Dixon 2009 Pittsburgh Steelers

Josh Johnson 2009 Tampa Bay Buccaneers

Pat White 2009 Miami Dolphins

Josh Freeman 2009 Tampa Bay Buccaneers

Joe Webb 2010 Minnesota Vikings

Thad Lewis 2012 Cleveland Browns

Cam Newton 2011 Carolina Panthers

Colin Kaepernick 2011 San Francisco 49er5s

Tyrod Taylor 2015 Baltimore Ravens

Terrelle Pryor 2012 Oakland Raiders

Robert Griffin 2012 Washington Redskins

Russell Wilson 2012 Seattle Seahawks

EJ Manuel 2013 Buffalo Bills

Geno Smith 2013 New York Jets

Teddy Bridge Water 2014 Minnesota Vikings

Jameis Winston 2015 Tampa Bay Buccaneers

Dak Prescott 2016 Dallas Cowboys

Jacoby Brisset 2016 New England Patriots

Brett Hundley 2017 Green Bay Packers

Deshaun Watson 2017 Houston Texans

Deshone Kizer 2017 Cleveland Browns

Patrick Mahomes 2017 Kansas City Chiefs

Lamar Jackson 2018 Baltimore Ravens

Kyler Murray 2019 Arizona Cardinals

Dwayne Haskins 2019 Washington Redskins

PJ Walker 2020 Carolina Panthers

Jalen Hurts 2020 Philadelphia Eagles

Justin Fields 2021 Chicago Bears

Trey Lance 2021 San Francisco 49ers

Jordan Love 2021 Green Bay Packers

Tyler Huntley 2021 Baltimore Ravens

Malik Willis 2022 Tennessee Titans

Bryce Perkins 2022 Los Angeles Rams

Desmond Ridder 2022 Atlanta Falcons

Joshua Dobbs 2022 Tennessee

Anthony Brown 2022 Baltimore Ravens

Irony of Ironies

Eldrige Dickey was the first Black quarterback taken number one in the NFL draft in 1968 by the Oakland Raiders. Ken Stabler was taken in the second round that year by the Raiders.

In summer camp that year with the Oakland Raiders some observers felt that Dickey out played Ken Stabler but Dickey, even being the first draft pick, never got to throw a pass in a real game. He was told the all too familiar tale that he needed to change positions to wide receiver. At Tennessee State Eldridge threw for 6,523 yards and 67 touchdowns and was a three time All American. Yet why would the Raiders draft him number one in the first round and not give him a shot to play quarterback? In the late 1960's there were people in Pro football who said behind closed doors that coaches and owners thought maybe a Black quarterback could not learn the playbook or could not lead a majority White team. Eldridge Dickey had an IQ in the 130's extremely bright yet did not get the opportunity. He was denied the job opportunity to show what he could do. There is really no other way to categorize this but blatant racism in the NFL directed at the Black quarterback.

Eldrige Dickey could throw a ball 70 yards in games and one time tested on a practice field how far he could throw the ball, chucked it 97 yards. An All American at Tennessee State where the irony of ironies he was coached by Joe Gilliam Senior. Joe Gilliam's dad of the Pittsburg Steelers. The Irony does not stop there. Joe Gilliam Sr. Was a tremendous quarterback in his own right. He was drafted by the

Green Bay Packers, but this pattern of denying Black quarterback's opportunities, he was asked to change his position from quarterback. This was a constant theme in Pro football in the 1960's. Joe Gilliam Sr. decided to forget playing football and go into coaching. He was an incredibly bright, erudite man. Yet even though he was a remarkable coach, he could not get big college coaching opportunities and he was relegated to coaching at small Black Colleges. Joe Gilliam Senior saw what a denied opportunity did to his son Joe Jr. with the Steelers. When his son was replaced at quarterback in Pittsburg.

When the Raiders changed their number one draft pick Eldridge Dickey to wide receiver, he lost interest in the game, he hung on to the Raiders for a couple of years but that was the end of his quarterback opportunity in the NFL.

To continue the sad list of ironies Joe Gilliam Sr. Was one of Dickey's coaches at Tennessee State. Too many times Black men playing quarterback were denied their true opportunity to play quarterback in the 1950's, 1960's, 1970's and into the 1980's. Eldridge Dickey deserved a chance. Dickey was a remarkably talented quarterback that just needed a chance to show his teammates and coaches what he could do, it was a chance he never got.

ELDRIDGE DICKEY
NO 10
OAKLAND RAIDERS

To me the poem "Like Royalty" by Joe Doherty fits Eldridge Dickey. *"Whoever and wherever you are in this life you deserve to be celebrated.*

Five or Six was the Number

Neither League, the American Football League or the National Football League was doing what they should have done to give African Americans the opportunities they rightly deserved to play Pro Football. On the surface one would think the AFL of the 60's would have been much better giving Blacks an opportunity to play professional football. The AFL was the underdog up-start league that was desperately trying to compete with the tried- and- true conservative NFL. The AFL was full of rebels with a cause. They were out to prove they were the equal of the old stodgy NFL. At first glance of the two leagues the AFL appeared more liberal more inventive, more willing to give Black players more opportunities. The AFL played wide open football; they threw the ball from anywhere on the field. They featured their quarterbacks and offenses. It appeared to be an anything goes league. But when you really delve into the numbers of the AFL and the NFL in the 1960's the number of Black players on each team seemed to have an average cap that they did not go over. Both leagues, the AFL and NFL in the 1960's averaged about 5 to 6 Black players on each team. It was whispered in the front office hallways and in closed door meetings with Pro football ownership and coaches of both leagues that there may have been an unwritten rule. Pro teams in the AFL or NFL would keep the number of Black Players on a Pro Roster around 5 or 6. It was something that was not talked about in the light of day but was most likely in secretive conversations in private offices or talk hidden away in hallways. There seemed to be quotas in the NFL and the AFL of how many Black players you could have on each team and that number, through unwritten rules a league collusion, seemed to be five or six.

Warren Moon
Bad Moon Rising

14

In college Warren Moon attended a two-year West Los Angeles College, few 4-year colleges showed any interest. But the University of Washington under legendary Coach Don James gave him an opportunity to play quarterback for the Huskies. His senior year Moon led the Washington Huskies to the PAC 8 Title and an invite to the Rose Bowl. He then led Washington to an upset over Michigan 27-20. Moon was named the game MVP. But Moon was not drafted by any NFL team to play quarterback. The main reason for the non-draft position for Warren Moon was the "so called quarterback experts" felt that he did not have a strong enough arm. So, Moon went to Canada and helped to lead his team the Edmonton Eskimos to five straight Grey Cups.

In his six seasons in the Canadian Football League Moon amassed 1,369 completions on 2,382 attempts for 21,228 yards (about twice the cruising altitude of a commercial jet) and 144 touchdown passes. Off those six years of productivity Moon was drafted by the Houston Oilers. How in the world could you have a weak arm and throw for over 21,000 yards (about twice the height of Mount Everest) in the Canadian League? It is much harder to throw the football in Canadian football because if you are unaware the Canadian football used in the CFL is much bigger than the football used in the NFL.

It is fatter, every time I held one it seemed like a zeppelin, longer, fatter, and more difficult to control. Then in 1985 the CFL adopted to a regulation size NFL football, but Moon had to throw the bigger football in Canada. Plus, he played on a field in Canada that was much larger. The Canadian football field is 150 yards by 65 yards. The American football field is 120 yards by 53 ½ yards. Plus playing in incredibly cold, windy difficult football situations. How could someone with a weak arm throw for that much yardage in Canada with all the aforementioned conditions that would make it tough for any quarterback to throw the ball. Once again regarding the quarterback so-called experts got it wrong. Moon had a tremendous passing arm that he proved repeatedly in the NFL.

Warren Moon's NFL career numbers were 49,325 yards passing with 291 touchdown passes. So much for a weak arm for this NFL Hall of Fame African American quarterback. Warren wore the correct number in the NFL No. 1. He could flat out throw the football. He was made to go the hard road to get to the NFL playing six years in Canada, but he did it, he proved the experts wrong! I think Warren's measured height was 6'3" but visually on the field he looked shorter than that. He was not really a runner. He was a stand in the pocket guy who could really push the ball down field. I think because Moon was a slight bit shorter than 6'3 and he was not a runner; coaches did not visualize him as strictly a prototypical NFL drop-back thrower which he was. He was a classic NFL drop back passer. Warren Moon finally made all the critics believers!

WARREN MOON
NO. 1
HOUSTON OILERS

Warren Moon's song to me would be "Bad Moon Rising" by Credence Clearwater Revival. *I see the bad moon a rising, I see trouble on the way, I see earthquakes and lightnin,"*

Andre Ware

An opportunity lost with the Lions

Andre Ware in 1990 was the first-round selection of the Detroit Lions. Ware went to the University of Houston where his junior year he threw for 4,699 yards and 46 touchdowns. He set 27 NCAA records and averaged 52 passes a game in the Houston run and shoot offense. He also was the first Black quarterback to win the Heisman Trophy. He was originally headed to Texas, but they told him that they would switch him to defense, and he would not play quarterback for Texas, so Houston College was his team. He had an incredible career at Houston. He put mind numbing numbers on the board as a quarterback. The Lions fans thought they had their quarterback of the future. But the Lions, for a reason that I don't understand, did not give Andre Ware the opportunity, his talent, and the numbers he put up deserved it. He spent four seasons with the Lions. His total stats with the Lions were as follows: played in 14 games and started in six games, threw 5 touchdowns and 8 interceptions for 1,112 yards. In 1992 Ware started three games and went 2-1 as a starter. It sure looks as if the Lions drafted Andre Ware to just put another Heisman Trophy winner on their roster along with Barry Sanders. They did not take the time to develop Ware. They did not give him near enough playing opportunities at quarterback to develop a Pro passing skill set. He came out of Houston in the run and shoot and that footwork for a quarterback is much different than footwork for a drop back Pro passer. Andre Ware had immense talent, size, athletic ability and was extremely bright about the game. If being fair and honest you must ask tough questions of the Detroit Lions. Why did they not invest more time and effort in making this exceptionally talented young man their quarterback of the future? The Lions did have a starting veteran African American quarterback in Rodney Peete. Pete was a fifth-round draft pick for the Lions, Ware was a first-round pick. When you look at Peete's numbers, he played five years with the Detroit Lions, and he was 21-26 as a starter. He threw 38 touchdowns with 49 interceptions. Peete was a very serviceable quarterback but certainly not seen as great. In Ware you had a young talent that had greatness in him, but it was never developed. So why wasn't this young African American quarterback given the development opportunities he deserved after being drafted number one by the Detroit Lions? You cannot say race because the Lions already had a starting Black quarterback in Rodney Peete. But you can say stupidity to not try to develop a remarkable college talent like Ware, he needed reps but did not get them. He needed tutoring but did not get it. I believe that if Andre Ware had been coached by someone like Bill Walsh, he could have become a tremendous NFL talent at quarterback. Andre Ware as a number one draft pick by the Lions and the first Black Heisman Trophy winner was denied his destiny at quarterback in this instance not because of race, I believe but by coaching incompetence by the Lions staff at the quarterback position. The Lion's coaching staff was lazy with Andre Ware, they knew he came out of the run and shoot in Houston. They knew the footwork was totally different for the quarterback in that offense compared to the typical pro-offense. They drafted him number one but did not give him the teaching, mentoring and the reps he needed to relearn the footwork in the NFL. The Lions had a diamond in the rough at quarterback but stupidly did not try and polish it. Andre Ware was not given his deserved fair opportunity in the NFL.

ANDRE WARE
NO.11
DETROIT LIONS

Andre Ware's song should be "One" by Three Dog Night. *One is the saddest experience you'll ever know, yes it's the saddest experience you'll ever know.*

It was not just Black Quarterbacks that were not given professional opportunities

16

Black Quarterbacks were not given the opportunities that they deserved throughout the history of the NFL until Doug Williams became the first Black quarterback to win a super bowl with the Washington Red Skins in 1988, Super Bowl XXII.

But other professional sports also had terrible struggles trying to integrate their teams and giving African Americans the opportunities that they deserved. It was not just Black quarterbacks that had such an exceedingly challenging time trying to earn a rightful living playing professional sports. In 1947 everyone knows the remarkable Jackie Robinson broke the color barrier playing for the Brooklyn Dodgers and the difficulties Mr. Robinson and his family had to endure.

Sparky Anderson, the Cincinnati Reds, and Detroit Tigers Manager, once said about baseball not integrating sooner, "we were stupid!" He thought of all the great baseball players that played in the Negro Leagues but were not allowed to play in the majors.

The NBA did not start to allow Black players into the league until 1950. The first, really there were three, Chuck Cooper with the

Boston Celtics in 1950, then Nate (Sweet Water) Clifton in 1950 with the New York Knicks (Nate left the Globetrotters to join the Knicks) and Earl Lloyd with the Washington Capitols.

American sports were extraordinarily slow in giving minorities their rightful opportunity to play football, basketball, and baseball. And slow to incorporate many great African American athletes into various Halls of Fame. Many players from the old Negro Leagues in professional baseball are still being denied the major league Hall of Fame like Cannonball Dick Redding. In the early 1900's Cannonball had streaks as a pitcher where he won 17 games in a row then another of winning 20 games in a row as a pitcher. In 1917 in the Negro Leagues Cannonball had a pitching record of 14-3 and 0.73 ERA. Redding then threw over 12 no hitters sometimes pitching in both games of a double header. His career lasted from 1911 to 1938. So, it was not just pro football that held down minorities, but baseball and basketball did also with all the players from the Negro Leagues not getting the recognition they deserved and not enough of them getting into the Hall of Fame just like the Black quarterback Donovan McNabb.

McNabb threw for 37,276 yards in the NFL and 234 touchdowns. He led his Eagles team to 16 comeback wins and 24 game winning drives. McNabb led the Eagles to four consecutive NFC East Division Championships, five NFC Championship games and one Superbowl. McNabb had nine playoff wins. He is tied for 12th most playoff wins in the NFL, tied with Hall of Famer Kurt Warner and Hall of Famer Jim Kelly. McNabb has more play-off wins than Dan Marino and Steve Young. Every NFL quarterback with nine playoff wins is in the NFL Hall of Fame. McNabb still ranks 9th all time in rushing NFL quarterbacks, with 3,549 yards, a 5.6 career average that ranks 5th best all-time in the history of the NFL. How can Donovan McNabb, one of the all-time great African American quarterbacks not be in the pro football Hall of Fame in Canton, Ohio? He should be. The question needs to be asked repeatedly until Donovan McNabb is in rightly and justly where he belongs.

Doug Williams owes Bobby Mitchell

The Washington Redskins NFL football franchise finally integrated (now known as the Commanders) September 30, 1962. Bobby Mitchell picked up in a trade from the Cleveland Browns, stepped on to the field at DC Stadium in Washington to be the first African American player along with John Nisby and Ron Hatcher to finally break the color line with the Redskins. But Bobby Mitchell was the true high profile Black star with the Redskins. The owner of the Redskins during their period of segregation was George Preston Marshall. Marshall went to a segregated High School and lived in a segregated section of West Virginia. He held the personal belief that White citizens in Washington DC did not like to watch African Americans play Pro Football. Washington DC built a new stadium for the Redskins. Pete Rozelle, the new commissioner of the NFL went to Marshall to pressure him to integrate his Pro team, the only one in the NFL in 1960 that was not allowing Black players to play. But the real pressure came from President John Kennedy. President Kennedy sent his secretary of the Interior to speak with John Preston Marshall. That talk was most direct. The new DC Stadium built for the Redskins was built in part with Federal money and Marshall was told if he did not integrate his team, they would not be able to step foot in the new stadium. With the pressure from the NFL Commissioner and President Kennedy, Marshall caved and on October 1, 1961, Bobby Mitchell lined up against the St. Louis

Cardinals in the new Redskins stadium. Doug Williams owed Bobby Mitchell a lot!

147 yards with 2 touchdowns and the Redskins won 24-14. Finally in 1961 the color barrier was broken with the Washington Redskins. The irony of ironies with Bobby Mitchell crashing through this color ceiling was very important. Bobby and many talented African American football players paved the way, Bobby Mitchell was a true trailblazer.

BOBBY MITCHELL
49
WASHINGTON REDSKINS

Bobby's Poem would be from **"If" by Rudyard Kipling.** If you can keep your head when all about you are losing theirs"

Kordell Stewart
Slash takes the Field

18

Kordell Stewart was very well known as an extremely talented quarterback who played for Colorado. On September 24, 1994, on National TV Kordell threw a 64-yard pass into the end zone for a touchdown and became an instant folk hero. In the 1995 Draft Kordell was drafted in the second round with a handshake deal in Pittsburgh. He would get an opportunity to compete for the starting quarterback position. That did not really happen. In 1995 the starting quarterback for Pittsburg was Neil O'Donnell. Kordell did not get many opportunities. He ran the ball 15 times and caught 14 passes for 2 touchdowns. He got his first pass attempt in 1995 against Cleveland and it went for a touchdown. Kordell was so exceptionally talented, he could play quarterback, wide receiver and running back. He could even punt the football. But he knew he could be a great starting quarterback. In the 1996 Pittsburgh football season he still did not get his promised chance at quarterback. Kordell could play so many offensive positions he had the nickname "slash." In 1996 the Pittsburg Steelers decided to play Jim Miller as starting quarterback. Miller did not work out, then the Steelers went with Mike Tomczak, still Kordell did not get a chance to start at the quarterback position.

Finally in 1997, Kordell Stewart was given the opportunity to start at quarterback for the Pittsburg Steelers, as he was promised long ago. In his first season as a starting quarterback in the NFL he led the Pittsburg Steelers to a 11-5 record. Kordell was the first NFL quarterback in the history of the league to throw for 20 passing touchdowns and run for ten touchdowns in a single season in the history of the NFL.

In the year 2000 Kordell Stewart was replaced at quarterback by Kent Graham. Graham got hurt and Kordell took over and led the Steelers to a 9-7 season and missed the playoffs by one game. In 2001 Kordell is named the Pittsburg Steelers starting quarterback. Kordell was fantastic, he led the Steelers to a 13-3 record and into the play-offs. Kordell threw for 3000 yards, 14 passing touchdowns and ran for 5 more touchdowns. He led his Steelers to the AFC championship game. Kordell was named to the Pro Bowl as a quarterback and was voted Pittsburgh MVP.

You would think that Kordell Stewart had finally won some stability at the quarterback position in Pittsburg, but this was not the case. Early in the next season Kordell threw an interception against the Cleveland Browns and their all-pro MVP quarterback was replaced at the quarterback position by Tommy Maddox and released by the Pittsburgh Steelers at the end of the season. Kordell was a victim of his own extreme talent and broken promises by the Steelers.

Kordell Stewart should have had a long run at quarterback for the Pittsburgh Steelers. But he had so many talents and was used as a wide receiver, wideout, running back and quarterback; the Steelers had him do everything but park cars at the stadium. They should have concentrated on his quarterback skills and developed them, then they would have had a great starting quarterback for many years. Kordell was slashed by the Steelers. Kordell did not put up enough numbers for the Pro Football Hall of Fame yet Canton should have a separate exhibit for the "Slash" he was that special. No one like him in the history of pro football.

KORDELL STEWART
10
PITTSBURGH STEELERS

Kordell Stewarts song would be by Guns and Roses lead guitar, Slash, November Rain. *"Nothing lasts forever, and we both know hearts can change and it's hard to hold a candle in the cold November rain"*

19

What Should Have Been But Never Was

Michael Vick played 13 Pro Football Seasons for 4 different teams. He threw for 22,464 yards and 133 touchdowns. He was selected to play in 4 Pro Bowls and won one comeback Player of the Year.

Coming out of Virginia Tech, Vick posted the fastest 40-time for any quarterback in the history of the NFL 4.3. Michael was so very quick it was mind boggling it was hard to understand how a human being could be that fast in full gear on a football field. Vick looked like a cartoon character "The Flash" as his stride and his steps were so much quicker than the other players that he was on the field with. Vick had remarkable arm strength to go along with feet that seemed to belong to the "Silver Surf" gliding through secondaries, riding a wave into the end zone that no one else could. It appeared that it was going to be a Hollywood Career Story for the uniquely talented NFL quarterback, until Vick was found out to be part of a dog fighting ring. This egregious lack of judgement really for all practical purposes ended his career. That should have been a Hall of Fame career. I do not think there has ever been a quarterback in the NFL with Michael Vick's combination of unworldly foot speed and powerful arm strength but when you are a top draft pick at quarterback, and you are the face of the city and the football franchise that you represent you cannot make those types of decisions. You are a team leader.

People that sit in the stands or watch pro football on TV don't really understand how important character is at the quarterback position. You don't need to be a bible toting, church going, milk drinking boy scout to lead a pro team at quarterback. But you must have the respect of your teammates to lead them. Vick lost that and then lost his career.

MICHAEL VICK

7

ATLANTA FALCONS

Michael Vick's song...."Trouble ahead, trouble behind and you know that notion just crossed my mind" by Casey Jones of the Grateful Dead.

The Beatles Indirectly Helped Black Athletes and John Lennon's Death was announced to the World during Monday Night Football

When the Beatles came to America, in 1964, they took a stand on civil rights. They refused to perform at a segregated concert at the Gator Bowl in Jacksonville, Florida. The Beatles told the Jacksonville Community they would not play unless both Black and White audiences were allowed to go to their concert. John Lennon said, "We never play to segregated audiences and we aren't going to start now." Lennon also said, "I'd sooner lose our appearance money." So indirectly the Beatles made an extraordinarily strong statement about civil rights. And that in turn surely helped African Americans that were trying to make their way in the NFL Professional Sports in America.

I'm not saying that they solved any civil rights problems in the United States in the mid 1960's but what they did do is maybe, just maybe helped some people to rethink their position on integration and civil rights.

John Lennon was a major fan of Pro football and even made an appearance in the Monday Night Football booth with Howard

Cosell. On Monday Night Football, December 9, 1974, Howard Cosell interviewed John Lennon at half-time of the LA Rams vs Washington Redskins game.

Tragically and ironically years later John Lennon's death was announced December 8, 1980 in front of a live audience of millions as the Monday Night Football game was going on. Frank Gifford, the play-by-play announcer for ABC's Monday Night Football said to Howard Cosell, "I don't care what is on the line Howard, you have to say what we know in the booth." Howard said, "yes, we have to say it, remember this is just a football game, no matter who wins or loses. An unspeakable tragedy has been confirmed to us by ABC News in New York City, John Lennon, outside of his apartment building on the West side in New York City, the most famous perhaps of all the Beatles, was shot twice in the back, rushed to Roosevelt Hospital, and pronounced dead on arrival."

So, John Lennon and the Beatles had a tragic connection to United States Football and maybe, just maybe made some American football fans see that in the 60's race relations had to ameliorate in America, with the Beatles refusing to play to segregared audiences in the South. This important gesture may have caused some people in America to rethink race issue in the US in the 60's.

JOHN LENNON
9

John Lennon recorded a song called Number 9. *"You say you want a revolution; well you know we all want to change the world. You tell me that its evolution, well you know we all want to change the world"*

Lennon's song Number 9 was him just saying the Number 9 over and over again. Some NFL quarterbacks that wore Number 9:

Tony Romo
Carson Palmer
Jim McMahon
Sonny Jurgensen
Steve McNair
Drew Brees
Matthew Stafford
Joe Burrow
Ralph Guglielmi

Sonny Sixkiller best number and name in all of College and Pro Football

Sonny Sixkiller had the best quarterback's name ever in the history of college football or even Pro Football. He was a Cherokee Indian from Tahlequah, Oklahoma. He was not African American, but he experienced some of the prejudices that African American quarterbacks faced in college and Pro Football in the 1960's, 1970's and 1980's. Sixkiller's real first name was Alex, but he got his name Sonny from his grandmother who called him sonny all the time. The last name, Sixkiller, was a Cherokee surname. Some overzealous Rockwellian sportswriter printed a story that Sonny's last name, Sixkiller, came from his father or grandfather killing six bison, but that was not true.

In college Sixkiller, at Washington University, did not get the starting job because he did not look like a starting quarterback according to some at Washington. He was 5'11, long hair with Cherokee features. The quarterback that was beating him out was 6'3 Bond hair and had the look of a Hollywood image of a quarterback. Sixkiller did not. But that starting quarterback got hurt and Sonny Sixkiller finally got his chance to play and play he did. He was electric.

Sonny in three years at Washington University threw for 5,496 yards and 35 touchdowns. He was Superman with a big Washington "W" on his chest, able to leap over defenders in a single bound and throw over the top of tall buildings. He should have been drafted in the NFL, but they overlooked him because he was under six foot. Sonny could have been a star in professional football if given the right opportunity in the right system with a coach who could have created an offense that would have given Sixkiller passing windows. He was a truly gifted quarterback. Prejudice at the quarterback position did not just happen because of ethnicity in Sixkiller's case it was size.

Sixkiller got a free agent tryout with the Los Angeles Rams, but it did not work out. He had true star power and incredible quarterback passing skills. Doug Flutie fought the size issue his entire career in college and the Pro's, and he should be in the Pro Football Hall of Fame.

Sonny went on and did some sports broadcasting and also got a part in the Burt Reynold's movie in 1974, "The Longest Yard." Burt Reynolds who was a football player at Florida State with Lee Corso also claimed to be part Cherokee. Burt Reynolds and Lee Corso were roommates at Florida State.

Sonny Sixkiller was not African American; he was Cherokee Indian but none the less he was not given the opportunities at the quarterback position in the Pro's because of his lack of size and looks which begs the question what should a starting quarterback in college or Professional Football look like? There should be no look test, it should be if you can play or not and Sonny Sixkiller could play!

SONNY SIXKILLER

6

WASHINGTON UNIVERSITY

Sonny's song by Paul Revere and the Raiders. *"They took the whole Cherokee Nation, put us on this reservation, took away our ways of life"*

The Strange case of Donovan McNabb, Tums Anyone?

I made a case earlier in *Black in the Pocket* that Donovan McNabb should be in the Canton Pro Football Hall of Fame. He has the resume as I stated but one strange event that happened that haunts Donovan, even today, occurred in Super Bowl XXXIX, Eagles vs Patriots. Donovan McNabb was leading another one of his classic comebacks against the Patriots as the clock was running at the end of the game. It has been rumored that Donovan threw up on the potential game winning drive and that he could not call the plays in the huddle because he could not breathe. The accusation by Eagles fans was that Donovan was not in good shape, not conditioned the way he should have been. There is no video evidence of Donovan getting sick on the last drive, with over 100 cameras on the game. If that happened in Super Bowl XXXIX it would have been caught on video. It is not there. Eagles' fans needed to blame someone; they needed an excuse. Remember these fans used to throw wine bottles at Santa Claus on Christmas in the Old Veteran Stadium. The Eagles fans were so bad they put a court underneath the stadium and they would bring the unruly fans right in front of the judge at the game. Some say Donovan got sick at the end of the game because he was nervous. A quarterback does not get a nervous stomach in the fourth quarter of a game. It is before the game starts, not at the end. McNabb took a couple of big hits on the last attempt at a game winning drive in the Super Bowl against the Patriots. He had trouble breathing and talking, that is real, that happens. It has nothing to do with conditioning. I believe this false narrative about a great African American quarterback has hurt his case to get into the Pro Football Hall of Fame. Donovan deserves better. He just came up a little short in Super Bowl XXXIX against the Patriots.

DONOVAN MCNABB

5

PHILADELPHIA EAGLES

Donovan's song....Don't Let me down by the Beatles. "Don't Let me down, don't let me down, don't let me down, don't let me down.

The Eagle fans and some of his teammates let Donovan Down.

Lombardi Stands Up, Lombardi never saw Color

When Vince Lombardi became the head coach of the Green Bay Packers from 1959 to 1967, he changed everything about race on his football team. He took over a terrible football franchise in Green Bay. Lombardi made it very clear that the players were going to work harder than they had ever worked in their lives and that was not a canard. He pushed his players to their limits and beyond. He also challenged his players on the race issue in pro football and on his team. Coach Lombardi told his players no form of racism would be tolerated on his Packers Team. He let a number of Packers go because they broke his code on race and his team. No room assignments for the Packers were to be made on skin color. Black and White players roomed together, that was part of Coach Lombardi's plan. One of the first things that Lombardi did was acquire a great Black football player from the New York Giants, Emlen Tunnell. Emlen played for eleven years for the Giants and played for Coach Lombardi when he coached in New York. Emlin held the NFL record for interceptions at 74. Coach Lombardi also made Emlin an assistant coach on the Packers plus hired him as a scout.

Lombardi also went to all the restaurant owners and bar owners in Green Bay and told them if they ever denied service to any of the

Black Packer Players, the entire Green Bay Football Team would boycott their places. Coach Lombardi also helped to pass a Fair Housing Bill in Wisconsin so that minorities could buy homes. In 1962 Lombardi refused (like the Beatles did) to play a game in Columbus, Georgia against Washington because of a segregated seating plan at the game. Coach Lombardi stood up and made a difference in race relations in pro football and life.

VINCE LOMBARDI
40
FORDHAM UNIVERSITY

Vince Lombardi wore this number at Fordham, he was one of the legendary "Seven Blocks of Granite."

A John F. Kennedy statement perfectly portrays Coach Lombardi's view of race. "It ought to be possible in short, for every American to enjoy the privileges of being American without regard to race or color."

Encouraging the Black Quarterback to Run

One of the reasons the African American quarterback has had difficulty in developing and maintaining a starting position in the NFL is because very often the African American quarterback was viewed by coaches and team management as an outstanding overall athlete. therefore, encouraged to run and the Black Pro quarterback had a good deal of success running with the football. Whereas the majority of the White quarterbacks were seen as pocket throwers and encouraged to stay in the pocket and work from the pocket. NFL offenses were designed for the White quarterback to stay in the pocket. What has happened to too many Black players in the NFL is that it was demanded that they use their legs, their athleticism to make plays to get out of defensive pressure. The problem with that is most times to be successful at the quarterback position in the NFL you must throw the ball on time, get it in and out of your hands, there is a rhythm to it. If you are running around all over the field the football is not coming out on time and the worst part of the running is that you are going to take way too many hits. Those hits when you are running out of the pocket do damage to the quarterback, a great deal of damage. Case in point, Justin Fields playing for the Steelers. He is such an incredible athlete he was encouraged to make plays with his legs, not work on beating a team from the pocket. He should be discouraged from running and absolutely encouraged to set-up and throw the ball on time from the pocket. Any quarterback that relies too much on running in the NFL, the NFL acronym (Not for Long) applies. To be successful in the NFL as a quarterback you have to learn to operate out the premise "get the ball out of your hands on time and do not take any unnecessary hits. The Black quarterbacks were always asked to use their legs and run more to the detriment of their own personal and professional development.

JUSTIN FIELDS

1

PITTSBURGH STEELERS

Justin Fields song Run, Run, Run by JoJo Gunne. *"Oh, welcome to the party, we're all just papers in the wind, run, run"*

What If?

What if Bill Walsh got the head coaching position in 1978 in San Francisco instead of 1979? In 1978 if Bill had that job, he very likely would have drafted Doug Williams. If Williams had the opportunity to be tutored by "The Great One" Bill Walsh, history could have been quite different. Doug Williams could have won a Super Bowl much earlier. And if Doug Williams had won a Super Bowl earlier, if he was coached by "the Genius" Bill Walsh the timetable for other African American quarterbacks moves up significantly. So many people do not truly understand the elements that are necessary to allow a Pro Quarterback to be successful. To become an outstanding Pro Quarterback, you need first "coaching." You need a coaching staff that understands their quarterback's skill set and puts an offense around him that fits the quarterback's skills. Maybe he is a deep ball thrower, so you need to establish a tremendous offensive line with speed receivers on the outside, to create deep ball opportunities. Maybe your quarterback is a short to mid-range very accurate thrower. Then you need to have a strong running game that he can play action off of and hit shorter routes, 10-18 yards after a good running play fake. Every developing Pro Quarterback needs a solid defense so that he does not have to play from behind all the time. When a quarterback has to play from behind all the time, he will get sacked often because the defense knows he has to throw, and they are coming after him. Let's continue the game of "what if." Let's talk about Joe Montana, for my money the greatest quarterback that ever played in the Pro Game. Super Joe was 4-0 in Super Bowls.

Brady lost two and should have lost three if the Seahawks don't make a very dumb call on the goal line. Joe's style, his footwork, passing arc were all exemplary. His poise, his courage under duress was remarkable. He could throw both long and short passes, but Bill Walsh tailored an offense perfectly to fit Joe Montana's skill set. He also did not have Joe start right away because early on San Francisco was not a good football team. Walsh knew this so he would start Steve Deberg, a veteran quarterback to quarterback those tough games where San Francisco was out classed. Deberg would take the beatings and the losses. Then when there was a chance for San Francisco to win a game and compete he would put Montana in the game. Montana would do well, and the team would see him being successful and they would also see him leading. Walsh would also give Montana the first fifteen plays that he would call to start the game. Walsh always picked the plays that Joe threw best. It gave him true success and a lot of confidence. Do not misinterpret, Tom Brady is a remarkable Pro Quarterback, but he went to a team that had a great head coach, Bill Belichick of the Patriots. Belichick also understood that to make a young quarterback successful that quarterback would need a strong defense to support and certainly a solid offensive line with some talented runners and receivers. For just about all of his career in New England Tom Brady had all those things. When he brought his skills to Tampa Bay he went to a tremendously talented team, both defensively and offensively. Tom Brady knew what it took to be successful at the quarterback position.

So, playing the "what if" game, if Doug Williams had been drafted in 1978 by Bill Walsh, if he had the job in 1978, not 1979 I certainly believe that Doug Williams would have become the first Black quarterback to win a Super Bowl much earlier than he did in 1988 with Washington. And if that had happened more African American quarterbacks in the NFL might have gotten their chances much earlier! What if?

JOE MONTANA
16
SAN FRANCISCO

Joe Cool's song would be by Hue Lewis and the News. *"They tell me that it's good for me but I don't even care, I know that its Crazy, I know that it's nowhere, it's hip to be square"*

Joe Montana and his teammates were big fans of Huey Lewis and the News.

Doug and Joe
A Gut Feeling and the Long Ball

Doug Williams and Joe Gibbs are linked together forever and together they change the landscape in Pro Football for the Black quarterback. In 1978 Doug Williams, out of Grambling College, was drafted Number 1 by the Tampa Bay Buccaneers. He was the first African American quarterback to be taken in the first round. Gibbs at that time was the offensive coordinator for Tampa Bay and one of their key scouts. Gibbs had a job as a scout for Tampa to find the Buccaneers a starting quarterback. Gibbs found that Williams was teaching school in Monroe, Louisiana. Gibbs went to see Doug and sat in the back of his classroom, then after class they went to McDonalds together. Joe Gibbs was so impressed by Doug's intelligence. He had incredible knowledge and understanding of the game. Williams also possessed a big-time arm and Gibbs sensed that Doug was also extremely tough. Gibbs knew how important that was in the NFL. So, Joe Gibbs got back to the Tampa Football officials and said we have to draft Doug Williams. So, Tampa drafted Doug Williams Number 1 with the 17th pick in the draft of 1978. Doug Williams became the starting quarterback in Tampa and Joe Gibbs went to the Washinton Redskins to become their head coach.

Doug Williams had an excellent career in Tampa. Doug threw for 12,648 yards and 73 touchdowns and 73 interceptions in Tampa. In

1981, Williams led the Buccaneers to a division title and a berth in the NFC Championship Game. He also led the Buck's to an above 500 record for his final four seasons in Tampa.

In 1987 with Joe Gibbs as head coach of the Washington Redskins he traded to get Doug Williams from the USFL and Tampa Bay. Williams was brought in to be a back-up for Jay Schroeder. In 1987, in the midst of a Super Bowl run, quarterback Jay Schroeder, of the Redskins was hurt often. Joe Gibbs decided to replace Schroeder with Doug Williams because the times that Doug did get into the game, he had an incredible quarterback rating of 94.0 and Williams did the rest, he took the Redskins to an amazing victory in Super Bowl XXII as they routed John Elway and the Denver Broncos, 42-10. Doug became the Super Bowl MVP, connecting on 18 of 29 passes for 340 yards, 4 touchdowns and one Interception, a truly remarkable performance.

But the Doug Williams – Joe Gibbs Story was much more than just the Super Bowl Game. Those were two men who had great loyalty and respect for one another. Joe Gibbs, every opportunity he got, incorporated Doug Williams into his own family, having Williams over to his house many times for dinner.

One event at Tampa tells what the entire relationship between Doug and Joe was all about. Doug Williams had a quarterback coach in Tampa, who will remain nameless, but verbally attacked Williams on the field in front of the other Buccaneer players. The criticism went way beyond coaching, it got personal. Joe was also an assistant coach at Tampa at the time. He sprinted all the way across the field, got in the face of the quarterback coach that was verbally attacking Doug Wiliams and told that coach in very direct language that he will never again do that to Williams, or he would answer to him, it did not happen again.

- TOM COLE -

JOE GIBBS

11

TAMPA BAY

Number 11 was the number Joe Gibbs wore on his Jersey at William & Mary College and also the number on his race car.

Joe Gibbs song would be Three Dog Night's Black and White. "*The ink is black the page is white, together we learn to read and write. A child is black, a child is white, the whole world looks upon the sight, a beautiful sight.*

Doug Williams could always throw the long ball and his head coach Joe Gibbs always had a gut feeling that Williams could take him to the World Championship. They both took that ride together!

Michigan State helped to Lead the Way

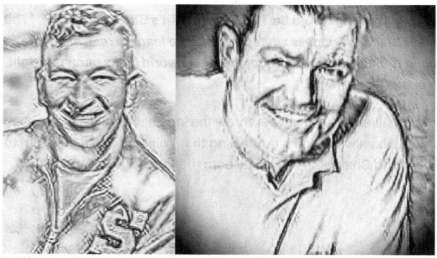

Duffy Daugherty   Darrell Royal

A year before the University of Texas made Julius Whittier its first Black varsity football player in 1970 Michigan State named Clifton R. Wharton its first Black president. That is how progressive Michigan State was integrating their campus. Another key person leading the way was Head Football Coach Duffy Daugherty. In 1965 and 1966 Duffy was able to lead Michigan State to back-to-back national championships. Daugherty not only recruited athletes from the State of Michigan but Ohio and Texas. Duffy recruited Black players that could have gone to the University of Texas. While Duffy was recruiting in Texas, he would run across Darrell Royal the Head

Football Coach in Texas, who had won national championships. Duffy had to have wondered in his mind with Texas being so full of athletic football talent why Darrell Royal did not recruit Black football players. In 1964 Darrell Royal, Head Coach at Texas was given the okay from the University of Texas to give football scholarships to Black athletes. How many did he give in 1964? Zero, 1965, zero, 1966 zero, 1967 zero, one in 1969 and one in 1970. Then in 1972 zero. In November of 1970, a reporter from Harper's Magazine asked Royal, "Is it important to you that you have Negro Players on the team?" Royal replied "No." Duffy Daugherty would not understand nor agree with that viewpoint.

Duffy Daugherty's 1966 Michigan State football team had twenty Black players on it with eleven African American football players that were starters. Coach Duffy Daugherty brought 59 Black players from the South to play at Michigan State from 1959 to 1972. Sixty-eight percent of those Black players received degrees from Michigan State.

President John F. Kennedy once said, "one man can make a difference, and everyone should try." Duffy chose the correct path on integration for Black athletes playing football. The Texas Head Football Coach did not. Darrell Royal chose to stick his head in the sand and not give fair opportunity, denying people progress. These two coaches both won multiple national championships but how you win is important. What you stand for is important. Daugherty's 19-year reign as Head Football Coach at Michigan State from 1954 to 1972 recorded a winning record of 109-69-5 plus two national championship teams. Duffey was only 5'7" but he stood so very tall, helping Black athletes get an education and a degree and be allowed to play college football. Duffy Daugherty was a "Giant!" Darrell Royal turned a blind eye to injustice because it was socially and politically difficult in Texas at that time, no excuse a coach should lead especially when it is difficult to do!

One Man's View

I have been truly fortunate to have coached high school and college quarterbacks for over 30 years. I really do not understand as a coach "why" or "how" a coach would tell a youngster because he is Black, Hispanic, Indian, or Asian that they could not play quarterback and that they needed to change positions. I can very honestly say that thought never ever entered my mind. It was never on the horizon, it was never mentioned to me by a head coach, high school, or college. It is hard to understand. Sports to me has always been the great equalizer as far as race is concerned. I don't understand in any way, shape, or form anything other than the best person plays, Black, White, or Brown makes no difference. It is awfully hard to understand how some powerful head football coaches in the South denied Black athletes and especially Black quarterbacks the chance to play. The Coaches that denied the Black athletes' opportunities, those coaches had to know in their heart of hearts that what they were doing, denying opportunities to athletes of color was wrong.

Darrell Royal, Head Coach of the University of Texas won three national championships and had a winning record of 167-47-5, but to me all his wins and national championships don't mean much when they stand next to his record on race. His record of giving Black athletes the opportunities to play football and receive an education that they justly deserved.

In 1970 Royal gave an interview to Harper's Magazine. Royal told the following story. "A bunch of negro boys came to me a while ago and said I could solve all possible difficulties by hiring a Black coach. Now that would be fine for them, but I've got to look at the other side. I'd have a lot of White boys on the team coming to me saying they couldn't play for a Black coach. The family atmosphere of the team would be destroyed. Once the club harmony and spirit begin to deteriorate, I don't care what kind of talent you have, you won't win." Royal finally hired a Black coach in 1971.

One of the reasons Royal retired is because he said he was viewed as a racist. He had to know in his heart what he had done was wrong. How you win matters, Darrell Royal got it wrong.

Hayden Fry
"The Coach"

John Hayden Fry was born February 28, 1929, and died December 17, 2019. He was a college football player and one of the most unique college football head coaches in the history of the game. He compiled a head coaching record of 232-178-10. Fry played quarterback at Baylor. As a coach he led the Iowa Hawkeyes to 14 Bowl games; he also led the Hawkeyes to three Big Ten titles and three Rose Bowl appearances. Fry painted the visitors' locker room in Iowa all pink. He thought that pink was a passive color, that it would affect the visiting team. He thought it would make them less aggressive. He developed a passing attack way before anyone else was throwing the football. When Fry was head coach at Southern Methodist University his quarterback, Chuck Hixon put up remarkable passing numbers from 1968 to 1970. In total Hixon threw for 7,179 yards and 40 touchdowns. Hixon also completed 1,115 passes. In this period in college football most teams were predominately running football, I.e., Ohio State with Woody Hays and Bo Schembechler at Michigan. Hayden was always different. He was never conventional; he never followed the trends. When he was at Baylor playing quarterback, he also earned a degree in Psychology. I think that is part of what made Hayden so vastly different than other head college football coaches. Hayden invented the stand-up tight end, no one had ever done that before. Hayden Fry was popular and such an impactful presence on the Iowa Campus on the football field and in the classrooms that a former Iowa alum, Barry Kemp, created a TV football coach named Coach Hayden Fox played by Craig T. Nelson, loosely based on Hayden Fry at Iowa.

But for all of Hayden Fry's remarkable head coaching accomplishments, Hayden Fry said the one thing he is most proud of is that he was the first coach in the history of the Southwest Conference to sign an African American football player to a scholarship. That player was Jerry Levias who became an Academic All American, plus an Athletic All American and earned his degree, that is what Hayden Fry was most proud of in his career.

HAYDEN FRY

17

BAYLOR UNIVERSITY

A poem for Coach Fry by Langston Hughes called "I Too." "*I too sing America, I am the darker brother. They send me to eat in the kitchen when company comes, but I laugh and eat well and grow strong. Tomorrow I will be at the table when company comes.*"

And, yes, if you were wondering the urinals were also painted Pink in the Iowa visitor's locker room.

In The Pocket

Since this book is all about the difficulties of Black Quarterbacks to get a fair opportunity to play the position in the 1960's, 1970's and 1980's I wanted to describe in this chapter what it was like to take a snap from center even though so many quarterbacks get the privilege of taking shotgun or pistol snaps today. It does not make any difference if you are Black, White, Hispanic, or Indian getting under the center, and taking a snap and dropping back five or seven steps, standing in the pocket, looking down field, and trying to find someone to throw the ball to is an incredibly difficult thing to do in sports. I think it is tougher than trying to hit a baseball, tougher than trying to shoot par on a particularly good golf course or to be a goalie in Hockey. I know that all the aforementioned are challenging and difficult but standing in the pocket in the 60's, 70's and 80's, in Pro Football was a bit of a testament of courage. Back in those days you were allowed to do anything to a quarterback, hit them, hit them late, hit them in the head, try to break an arm or a leg. Watch a film of the Oakland Raiders playing the New York Jets in the 60's and 70's and watch what the Raiders tried to do to Joe Namath. The way the game is played today the quarterback is in a protective bubble, he could play his position in shorts and t-shirts. It is a pass and tap today for Pro quarterbacks in Pro Football. You really cannot touch the quarterback in the pocket. But again, if you played the position in high school and college in the 60's and 70's, which I did, the name of the game was "get the quarterback" and hit him any way you can, high, low, or late, just intimidate him.

But in those really rough days of football when you dropped back to pass, and you were standing tall in the pocket you could hear the two lines hitting together. In the pocket you can feel the pressure. You can feel the hit coming even if you cannot see it. In the old days when a quarterback got hit from his blindside that is as brutal as it gets. It is like an Indy Race Car driver hitting a brick wall at full speed. Also, as a quarterback standing tall looking downfield sometimes it looks or feels like an old TV screen that has been turned off and the big picture starts shrinking very quickly, your vision gets, at times, a little blurry and a little cloudy. Then you can hear the breathing of the half-crazed defensive players that are trying to get to you to deliver a knockout blow. Google the blindside shot that Joe Montana took from the Giants, it would make you never ever even want to drop back and stand tall in the pocket. Being a quarterback regardless of color or race, back in the day, was a very dangerous place to be, today in pro football, not so much.

Tom Brady was able to play so many years in today's game because he was set up in an offense where he got the ball in and out of his hands very quickly and on top of that from the middle of Tom's career going forward you really could not hit the quarterback. As incredible as Brady was, he would never have had such a long career if he had played predominantly in the 1960's and 1970's. In the pocket in those days was no joke!

TOM COLE
10-14
MY OLD HIGHSCHOOL
AND
COLLEGE NUMBERS
AT
QUARTERBACK

Song for any QB that played football in the 60's and 70's and tried to stand tall in "the pocket." Stuck in the Middle with You by Stealers Wheel. *"Well I don't know why I came here tonight, I've got a feeling that something aint right. I'm so scared in case I fall off my chair and I'm wondering how I'll get down the stairs. Clowns to the left of me, jokers to the right. Here I am stuck in the middle with you!"*

The Tide Could Have Turned Early

Paul William "Bear" Bryant born September 11, 1913, is considered by many to be the greatest college football coach in America. During his 25 years as Head Football Coach at Alabama, he won six National Championships and thirteen conference championships. And, yes, he did wrestle a Bear as a young man and that is how he got his nickname Bear. He wrestled a Bear at a carnival for one dollar. The Bear bit his ear and Bryant survived but never got paid.

When Bryant got the head football job in 1954 at Texas AM he had inherited a team that was terrible. So, he decided to take 115 Texas A & M Football Players to an August double session summer camp in Junction, Texas. In the worst conditions anyone could imagine, temperatures in the high 90's (many times hitting 100 degrees), training on a football field with no grass, all dirt rocks and cactus. At night, no break from the heat, no air conditioning, and no water at practice except you could suck on a wet towel. Hitting was all day long with no breaks. There was limited medical attention, taking an aspirin was about the extent of it. During the Bear Bryant Junction practices one lineman almost died. They had to pack him in ice to keep him alive. Bryant would be in jail today if he ran Junction Double Sessions now. After the ten-day practices in this hell hole only 35 kids survived. The rest were run off by the brutality of Bear Bryant. That camp on toughness did nothing for Texas A&M, that season they finished 1-9. The next two years they did become winners and had a championship team.

After three years at Texas A & M Bryant got the call to go to Alabama as their head football coach. That is when his incredible legendary winning career in Alabama began. Bryant became more popular and more powerful in the State of Alabama than the governor, or any senator or congressperson or even the President of Alabama University himself. Bear had absolute power in the state. In 1963 a law was passed at Alabama University that said that Black and White athletes could now compete together on the same athletic fields. Bear Bryant waited until 1970 to give a Black player a scholarship to play football at Alabama. Bryant, with all the ultimate power that he had in the state of Alabama, could have integrated his team much sooner, and not wait seven years to do so. Bear Bryant was a remarkable leader, but he did not lead at all in social justice. He said that the political and social climate in Alabama was not ready for integration of its football team. That is a canard. A true leader with the kind of power that Bryant had would have pushed against that climate and so-called social norms and would do the right thing regarding integrating his team, unfortunately he did not.

Bear Bryant is considered one of the greatest college football coaches ever and he certainly deserves that title if you are just talking about wins, (323 wins) as a head football coach. Besides Bear's lack in pushing integration many of his brutal training techniques filtered down to other college coaches and high school coaches. They saw that Bryant won so he was the role model. Be tough, almost brutal, with your football kids and that will make them and you a winner. That is flat out not true. Football is a tough enough sport as it is, without trying to physically intimidate kids. It should be tough but fair, safety first, respect the health and well being of the kids you are in charge of as a coach; teach, instruct and motivate and inspire them don't beat them up.

The first Black quarterback to start at Alabama did not occur until 1980, to 1983. Walter Lewis started 44 games for Alabama. He threw for 4,257 yards and 29 touchdowns. He was named first team All Sec Conference quarterback.

WALTER LEWIS
10
ALABAMA

Walter's song is "Sweet Home Alabama" by Lynyrd Skynyrd. "In Birmingham they love the governor (boo, boo, boo!) Now we all did what we could do"

Cornelius Greene

32

Cornelius Greene was born January 21, 1954. He is the first African American quarterback to start for the Ohio State Buckeyes. Green accepted a football scholarship from Ohio State to play under Woody Hayes. As a sophomore he was named the starter at quarterback over Greg Hare. Green was an instant success. He was named Big Ten MVP for the 1975 season, when his teammate Archie Griffin, became the first two-time Heisman Trophy winner. Green compiled a 31-2-1 record as the starting quarterback during the regular season. He played in four Rose Bowls and won the 1974 Rose Bowl against the University of Southern California and won three Big Ten Championships. He also led the Ohio State team to an undefeated 1973 season. Although Greene's Ohio State teams under Woody ran the football more than they threw, Greene did well throwing the ball. In his career at Ohio State, he completed 138 out of 251 passes for 2,255 yards and 17 touchdowns. Running the ball Corny had 409 carries for 2,014 yards averaging 4.9 yards a carry and 28 touchdowns.

Corny Greene was an incredible quarterback at Ohio State. After college Corny was selected by the Dallas Cowboys in the 11th round of the draft. The 318th player chosen and overall, he had more upside potential at quarterback than most of the quarterback's taken ahead of him. Dallas did not even look at him as a quarterback and switched him right away to wide receiver. Many people believe that it is easy to switch from quarterback to wide receiver. It is not. Those are two vastly different positions. Somehow, I do not see Mahomes, Montana or Burrough having success in the NFL at wide receiver. I know it has been done but to me it is more of the exception than the norm.

If Cornelius Greene were playing in today's NFL, he would have been a top pick at quarterback. He would be a more explosive prototype of Lamar Jackson and as fantastic as Lamar is, Corny was a better runner and had the same throwing ability as Jackson. Lamar Jackson is not a perfect passer. His passing motion is elongated, he had too wide of a passing arc. He does not move his front foot to throw outside sideline throws, that is why sometimes his sideline throws sail. Yet he is one of the top 5 quarterbacks in the NFL. Corny had some of those less than fundamental passing habits; but I genuinely think if given the proper opportunity and reps Corny Greene could have been a standout NFL quarterback. But, unfortunately because of the unfortunate trend when he came out of college of not working with African American quarterbacks but immediately switching them to wide receiver, defensive back or running back, it was a lost opportunity.

Corny Greene did not get the chance at quarterback that he deserved. Tackling Corny Greene, when he dropped back in the pocket to throw, when his protection broke down, was a lot like dropping a thermometer on the ground, having it break and all the mercury spill out. You try to pick it up, but it is elusive, impossible, that was what it was like to try to tackle Cornelius Green, like picking up mercury. Cornelius Greene one of the most gifted talents to ever play quarterback at Ohio State and the Big Ten.

CORNELIUS GREENE
7
DALLAS

Song for Corny is "Catch us if you can" by the Dave Clark Five. *'Here they come again. Catch us if you can. Time to get a move on. We will yell with all of our might."*

Dennis Franklin

Michigan's First Black Quarterback

33

Dennis Franklin was born August 24, 1953. He played quarterback at Michigan from 1972 to 1974. He was recruited by Michigan after starring for the Massillon High School Football Team. Franklin is known as Michigan's first Black quarterback. With Franklin at quarterback, he led Michigan to three straight conference title ties with Ohio State. As their quarterback Dennis led Michigan to a record 30 wins and 2 losses and one tie. He also became first·team All Big Ten. Franklin's career passing stats at Michigan were 294 passing attempts, 153 completions and 18 touchdowns for 2,285 yards. His career rushing stats were 351 attempts for 1609 yards and 16 touchdowns.

Dennis was drafted by the Detroit Lions in the sixth round of the 1975 NFL Draft. The Lions then, instead of looking at his true quarterback abilities switched Dennis Franklin to wide receiver, a story that you hear repeatedly in the 60's and 70's in the NFL. His NFL career consisted of 9 games, 6 receptions for 125 yards. But I think Dennis may have ultimately gotten the last laugh. When he retired from football, he rose to the position of vice president at King World Productions in New York. They produced Wheel of Fortune, Jeopardy, and Oprah. Dennis Franklin was a true starting quarterback of television Productions; he did not need the NFL.

DENNIS FRANKLIN
9
DETROIT LIONS

Dennis Franklin's song is by Cory Heart called "Sunglasses." "I can't believe it. Don't be afraid of the guy in the shades, oh no, It can't escape you cause you got it made with the guy in the shades oh no"

Cliff Brown
Notre Dame

34

Clifton Brown was born June 14, 1952. He was the first Black quarterback to start a game for Notre Dame, after future Hall of Famer, Joe Theismann, graduated from Notre Dame in 1971. The Irish Head Coach Ara Parseghian selected Pat Steenberge to start the first two games; but he suffered a knee injury that ended his season. Then Bill Etter started the next two games, and he then also suffered a knee injury. At that point Cliff Brown got his chance. He appeared in his first Notre Dame game, filling in against Miami in the second quarter. Cliff led the Irish to a 17-0 victory. Brown started all the remaining games that season, losing only two games to USC and LSU. Cliffton Brown did an outstanding job filling in and taking over the starting quarterback position at Notre Dame and saving the season for the Irish. Cliffton quarterbacked his Irish to an 8-2 season in 1971. The next season he was replaced by Tom Clements, who in his own right was an outstanding quarterback, took over the job and Brown served as a back-up the next two years. When Cliff graduated from Notre Dame in 1974, he was drafted by the Eagles and switched to a running back position but did not make the team. You have to wonder when a third string quarterback comes in and saves your season, why they would not have a major leg up on the starting position. But that was not the case for Cliffton Brown, he was then relegated to back-up for the remainder of his career at Notre Dame. Cliff Brown was a true trailblazer at Notre Dame, being the first Black starting quarterback in the history of the school. To me No. 8 deserved a better fate.

CLIFTON BROWN
8
NOTRE DAME

Cliff Brown song, You Can't Always Get What You Want by the Rolling Stones. *"No you can't always get what you want. You can't always get what you want. But if you try sometimes you'll find, you get what you need"* **(Maybe an incredible ND education.)**

Tony Rice

Tony Rice was the first Black quarterback to lead Notre Dame to a National Championship. Tony Rice was born September 5, 1967, and is an American former professional football player who was a quarterback in the Canadian Football League and the World League of American Football. Rice is best remembered as a spectacular option quarterback at the University of Notre Dame and helped to lead the Irish to the 1988 National Championship under Hall of Famer Coach Lou Holtz. Rice played professional football for three seasons in the Canadian Football League with the Saskatchewan Roughriders and the Barcelona Dragons of the World League. He also played for the Munich Thunder in the Football League of Europe. He played quarterback on all those teams.

This great quarterback was passed up in the 1990 April draft by every team in the NFL. Why you ask? On the surface the question appears easier to answer. Rice was an option quarterback. The NFL did not use option quarterbacks then, they do today in many ways. The NFL has many RPO's that are run today. These plays are called "Run Pass Options." If Rice came out today with his unique skill set, there would be a place for him in the NFL. But there is a deeper reason among many that Black Athletic running quarterbacks were not given the opportunity to play at the highest level, the NFL. One of those reasons was time. The NFL coaches did not want to spend the time teaching Black running quarterbacks the fundamentals of the passing motion of the football and timing of the rhythm passing attack of Pro football. So, they opted for the easy way out and switched these standout quarterbacks to wide receivers, running backs and safeties. If Lamar Jackson had played college ball in the 60's and 70's he very likely, like Tony Rice, would not have been drafted. The NFL in the 60's, 70's and 80's had a very myopic view of the quarterback position, then you needed to be White and stand still in the pocket and throw the ball down field. Most in the NFL believed then and many still do today that you cannot win a Super Bowl in the NFL with a quarterback that runs around and makes plays with his legs. Patrick Mahomes has basically destroyed that theory forevermore, but too late for Tony Rice and other quarterbacks like him.

TONY RICE
9
NOTRE DAME

Tony's song is by JoJo Gunne... "Run, run, run, doo doo, doo, run, run, run doo, doo, doo"

36

Steve Young
The Anomaly

Steve Young was a great athlete that attended Brigham Young University. He struggled learning to throw the football as a traditional pocket passer, but he worked hard, improved, and had a tremendous season at Bigham Young University his senior year. He was a first-round draft pick of the United States Football League Los Angeles Express for an unheard of amount of money, 40 million dollars. The USFL eventually folded. One of Young's last games with the LA Express, his team all got on the bus to be taken to the stadium to the game and their bus driver refused to drive the team to the game unless he got paid cash up front. So, Steve Young and the team trainer had enough money on them to pay the bus driver and get to the game. When the USFL folded Steve Young was drafted by the Tampa Bay Buccaneers. They were a very poor team. Young had two so-so years there but then got the break of a lifetime. He was traded to the San Francisco 49ers to back maybe the greatest quarterback to ever play the game (sorry to the Brady people) Montana, but Montana never lost a Super Bowl Game and Brady lost two. And more importantly Young was to be tutored by the best quarterback coach in the history of professional football, Bill Walsh, and most likely the best offensive coordinator in the history of Pro Football and the best play caller ever in the Pro game. Steve Young caught the break of a lifetime as a quarterback. He sat behind Montana for four years then led the 49ers to three Super Bowl wins. Under

Bill Walsh, the guru of the modern passing game, Young limited his running and became a remarkable pocket passer.

But let's just say Steve Young were African American with his remarkable speed and athleticism, and his uncanny ability to run and you have to ask an important question and this is would Steve have been moved to a running back position and not be given the opportunity to develop into a pro football Hall of Fame quarterback. With the past undeniable history of Black athletic quarterbacks in the Pro game you would have to conclude that Steve Young would have been switched to a running back and would never have the time to develop.

STEVE YOUNG
8
SAN FRANCISO 49ERS

Song for Steve Young is The Gambler by Kenny Rodgers. *"And the night got deathly quiet and his face lost all expression, said, if you're gonna play the game boy, you gotta learn to play it right!"*

Black quarterbacks and the CFL

Bernie Custis was born September 23, 1928, he was an American and Canadian football player. He is known for having been the first Black professional quarterback in the modern era and the first in professional Canadian Football starting at quarterback for the Hamilton Tiger Cats in 1951. Bernie was drafted in 1951 in the eleventh round by the Cleveland Browns. The Cleveland Browns asked Custis to change positions and to play safety. Custis refused. They released him and he signed with the Hamilton Tiger Cats. Custis started at quarterback for the Hamilton Tiger Cats in 1951. His team finished 7-5 and made the play-offs. Bernie Custis was named to the Canadian League All Star Football Team as a quarterback. But as hard as it may be to understand, despite leading his team to the play-offs and being named an All Star, the following year Bernie Custis was switched to running back.

It really seems if you play quarterback and you are a great athlete who can also run you will get switched to another position, especially if you are African American. But it has happened to a few White quarterbacks. I had mentioned earlier the Steve Young story and it certainly needs to be stated that the Tim Tebow situation was very odd for the NFL. Tim Tebow was an incredible athlete, a strong runner, but it was said that he could not pass. That was really not true. They needed to set up a system that best suited Tim Tebow, a lot like the Ravens have done for Jackson. It is not the passing, but the type passes you ask a "Lamar Jackson" or "Tim Tebow" to throw.

But truth be told if you were a Black QB in the 60's and 70's in college and you were a great all-around athlete and a particularly good runner, odds are you are going to be asked to change positions, it was the way it was in that era of the NFL, there was no development of the Black athletic quarterback.

BERNIE CUSTIS
28
SYRACUSE UNIVERSITY

Bernie's song is by Deitrick Haddon called Baby Your a Star. *"Don't cha know who you are, Don't chu let anybody tell you nothin different, But you know what's in ya heart, Baby you're a star"*

Black QB's Hit Gold in Canada

The Canadian Football field is wider than the National Football League and the end zones are deeper. There was a higher priority in Canada for quarterbacks to be mobile to be able to run. The Canadian League Football in the 1960's, 1970's and 1980's was longer and fatter than the "Duke" (that's what they called the American football) that the NFL used. It was a much more difficult ball for quarterbacks to handle and throw. The modern Canadian Football Game today has basically copied the NFL Football; they are virtually the same size today.

Why did Black quarterbacks from the states have immediate success in Canada. Again, the fact the Black quarterback for the most part was a very good runner and running from the quarterback position was especially important in Canada because of the wider field. Black quarterbacks from the states were given more opportunities to develop at the quarterback position and not demanded that they change positions. They also developed their passing mechanics because the wider field made it more difficult to throw sideline cuts, it made you develop a stronger arm and a fundamentally solid passing release.

Black signal callers recognized their skills were not utilized in the National Football League, but the Canadian Football League presented a more attractive and realistic opportunity to showcase their talents. Many interconnected factors made Canada more attractive for Black quarterbacks. First, was the country's willingness to open its borders to quarterbacks "disenfranchised by American racism", said Karen Flynn, an associate professor of African American studies at the University of Illinois at Champaign-Urbana.

"The United States had this shameful history of slavery, KKK and Jim Crow. Canada on the other hand was more benevolent as a nation that welcomed fugitive slaves, free Blacks and loyalists via the Underground Railroad. "No doubt, quarterbacks who opted to play in Canada were somewhat aware of this narrative.

At least 82 African Americans have played quarterback in the CFL since 1958. The following are some of the American quarterbacks that were able to develop their skill set in the CFL; Damon Allen, Rick Foggie, Andre Ware, Spergon Wynn, Jarious Jackson, Roy Dewalt, Danny Barrett, J.C. Watts, Condredge Holloway, Chuck Ealey, Jimmy Jones, Tracy Ha, Cornelius Greene, Matt Reed, Karl Douglas and Sandy Stevens.

Canada was not perfect, but it was so much more open to giving American Black quarterbacks the opportunity to continue to develop their quarterback skills on a Professional basis without being asked to change to a wide receiver, running back or safety. Canada was much more accepting of the Black American Quarterback than America was.

Don't Denigrate Canadian Football

We have established that Canada as a country and as a football league with the (CFL) Canadian Football League was more liberal and more open to giving Black athletes opportunities to play professional football and giving American Black Athletes more chances to be a starting quarterback to lead a team and to be the face of a franchise than occurred back in the States. I have heard the NFL watch and turn their noses up and snicker a little when you mention Canadian League Football. That is completely incorrect. The CFL is an excellent professional football league. Yes, there are differences in the game with Canada using 12 players and forward motion is allowed and the field is wider, and the end zones are 20 yards deep. They also use just three downs instead of four. But do not let that fool you. Tune in and watch a CFL game and you will find it is incredibly fast paced. You will find there is tremendous team speed because you have to be able to run because the field is wider, you have more ground to cover. You will also find there are more Gash plays in CFL football. A Gash play being a play of over 20 more yards than in the NFL. I believe again the reason for that is the wider field, it is the spacing, there is more room to maneuver in the Canadian Game as opposed to the NFL Game. You will also find on average more deep passes completed in a Canadian League game on average than the NFL for a couple of reasons, more space and room to operate for the wide receivers and the back end of the CFL defenses being their safeties are not as solid as the safeties in the NFL. Plus, the NFL has changed a lot of their pass plays to be check down plays, not pushing the ball downfield. The CFL checks down less than the NFL and pushes the ball down field more. So, the next time you run into a Canadian League Game on your sports channel, watch it closely and you will see what excellent quality that the game really is. Also recognize and appreciate that Canada gave African American quarterbacks many more opportunities that they would get in the States in the 1960's, 1970's and 1980's.

The Canadian League also developed many White quarterbacks that honed their game in the CFL because the NFL did not want them. Many of those CFL White quarterbacks eventually got to the NFL and became tremendous players like Doug Flutie, Warren Moon, Jeff Garcia, Joe Theismann, and Vince Ferragamo. Don't sleep on the Canadian Football League, it is quality, exciting, fast paced football and give it the respect it deserves for giving Black American Athletes opportunities that the NFL did not. Don't knock the CFL.

Can You Teach Passing Mechanics?

Can you teach passing mechanics? The answer to that question is yes! It has been played out time and time again in the history of professional football. The talented Black quarterback, because many times he was very athletic, with excellent running ability and speed, they were not given in the 1960's, 1970's and 1980's the opportunity to develop the necessary drop back passing skills from the pocket to be successful in the NFL. It was easier for NFL coaches and owners to say the Black quarterback did not have the needed pocket passing skills to succeed so they did the easy thing. That was to tell them they needed to switch to wide receiver or running back or safety. But the easy way was not to me, the correct way. I have taught quarterback skills for over 30 years to high school and college quarterbacks. You can teach passing skills. Quarterback passing skills are all about footwork and understanding the passing arc. The passing arc is holding the football at sternum level and creating a small passing circle. Joe Namath, Joe Burrough and Warren Moon all have perfect passing circle motions. The footwork is vital. So very often you throw with your feet being right and balanced, you throw very often with your legs. These are all things that can be taught. It is repetition and muscle memory. It is also creating success for your quarterback. Understanding what passes that your quarterback throws well and then build from that. As great as Joe "Cool" Montana was Bill Walsh took passes out of the 49ers offense that Joe did not throw well. One of those passes was the deep post. The plays that you call for a quarterback will have a lot to do with his success or lack thereof.

All of the quarterback skills can be taught, can be learned, can be improved. This takes time, it may take a year or two with very intense quarterback tutoring. But NFL coaches and NFL owners did not want to put in the time to possibly develop a very talented quarterback. They just quickly gave up on the athletic quarterback and just said let's play him somewhere else and let's look for another quarterback. When the very talented quarterback for their franchise was right there under their noses. Yes, you can develop passing skills from the quarterback position. It is just that the NFL coaches and owners choose not to do that, big mistake, and they miss out on so many potential great quarterbacks. Teach, train, instruct and encourage and your QB's will through solid repetitions get better.

The Curious Case of Warren Moon

Harold Warren Moon played quarterback for 23 seasons professionally. He spent most of his career with the Houston Oilers of the NFL, and the Edmonton Eskimos of the Canadian Football League. In the NFL Moon also played for the Minnesota Vikings, Seattle Seahawks and the Kansas City Chiefs. Moon's NFL stats were 291 touchdowns, 49,325 passing yards and 22 rushing touchdowns. Moon's stats in the CFL were 144 touchdowns, and 21,228 in passing yards.

Warren played college football at Washington under the great Don James. His senior year he led Washington to a PAC 8 Title and a 27-20 win over Michigan. Moon was named the Rose Bowl's MVP. Warren's college stats at Washington University were as follows: completed 254 passes for 3,465 yards and 20 touchdowns. Despite his outstanding quarterback success at Washington Warren Moon went undrafted in the NFL. How could this prolific passer have no interest by the NFL? And Moon was not a runner, he was a pure pocket passer. He had a beautiful passing motion and compact arc. He was a ready-made pocket thrower. Yet again no interest from the NFL. You ask yourself the question why not? Then you must ask the next obvious question, if Warren were White when he came out of college at Washington would it have been a different story. Moon was a ready-made passer and needed no fundamental work on his passing abilities.

Moon then had to go to Canada. He signed with the Edmonton Eskimos. He went on to win 5 straight Grey Cup Championships. The Grey Cup is the Super Bowl of Canadian Football. Moon won the Canadian Super Bowl, leading his team at quarterback in 1978, 1979, 1980,1981 and 1982. This was an incredible accomplishment for Moon, his coaches, and teammates. Moon became the first Professional quarterback to throw for 5000 yards in 1982. Moon's final season in the CFL he threw for 5,648 yards. Moon's six years in the CFL he amassed 1,369 completions on 2,382 attempts for 21,228 yards and 144 touchdowns. He also was put in the CFL Hall of Fame.

When he decided to enter the NFL, he was signed by the Houston Oilers. In 1990 Moon led the NFL and the Houston Oilers and the entire league in passing. He threw for 4,639 yards. He also led the NFL in completions, 362, and touchdowns with 33. Also, in 1990 Moon threw for 527 yards in a game against Kansas City on December 16, 1990, the second highest single passing game in the history of the NFL at that time. Moon moved on from Houston and spent time in Minnesota and the Sea Hawks quarterback and ended his career in Kansas City with the Chiefs.

Warren Moon's combined passing numbers in the NFL are absolutely mind boggling. He had 3,988 completions for 49,325 yards and 291 passing touchdowns. Moon is also in the Pro Football Hall of Fame. A 23-year Pro quarterback career, two Pro Football Hall of Fames, CFL and the NFL. It still begs to question how this fantastic young quarterback, out of Washington University went undrafted by the so-called NFL experts. Moon did not have to be fixed. His passing motion was compact and had a perfect circle to it. He was not a running quarterback; he was a pure ready-made pocket passer. Maybe the NFL experts, in picking quarterbacks, thought he was too slight of build, but they were also wrong about that. He played 23 years as a fantastic Pro quarterback who operated out of the pocket. It is truly a curious and very questionable case of why Warren Moon was not drafted out of college to the NFL.

WARREN MOON
1
HOUSTON OILERS

Warren's song is "Tell Me Why" by the Beatles. *"Tell me why you cried and why you lied to me. Tell me why you cried and why you lied to me. Well, I gave you everything I had but you left me sitting on my own. Did you have to treat me, oh so bad? All I do is hang my head and moan. Tell me why you cried and why you lied to me. If there's something I have said or done, tell me what and I'll apologize.*

First Black Quarterback in the History of LSU

Carl Otis Trimble, from 1974 to 1976, was the first Black quarterback in the history of Louisiana State University. Just for a little background on athletic integration at LSU, the first Black wrestler was Joe Lee Lott, in 1971. The first Black basketball player was Collis Temple Jr. In 1974. The first Black cheerleaders were Ladeta Crowley and Herman Harris in 1975. The first Black volleyball and women's basketball player was Joanette Batiste Boutte in 1975.

But Carl Otis was the first Black quarterback to take a snap under the center at LSU 1974-1976. Carl was the first Black quarterback in the history of LSU. He played the first year of 1974 alternating time at quarterback. Then in his last two years at LSU he was switched to running back. When he graduated from LSU, he was headed to law school but tragically Carl never got that chance. He died in a swimming accident before he got that opportunity. He was extremely popular and well liked on campus and an exciting player to watch.

CARL OTIS TRIMBLE

3

LSU

Prayers to a student athlete who made a difference in his school and his community.

43

First Black Quarterback in the History of Wisconsin

Wisconsin became the first Big Ten Program to field a Black quarterback when Sidney Williams Jr., took that job from 1956 to 1958. Sidney Williams, who had rarely seen the field as a defensive back at Wisconsin was switched to quarterback in 1956. Sidney took his first snap against Illinois in 1956 and became the first African American starting quarterback in the modern era of the Big Ten. Williams' 9-yard touchdown run helped get the Badgers a 13-13 tie at Illinois. Then in 1957 Sidney Williams started every game at quarterback for Wisconsin. He helped to lead the Badgers to a 6-3 record and a number 19 ranking in the Associated Press Poll.

Williams left Wisconsin in 1958 to play two years of Professional football, one in the NFL and one in Canada. Sidney did get injured playing professional football and decided to give it up. He returned to Wisconsin University and received a degree in chemical engineering. He also went on to receive a law degree from George Washington University in 1967. Sidney was elected into the Wisconsin Athletic Hall of Fame in 2008.

So, certainly kudos to the University of Wisconsin Football program for having the foresight to give an opportunity to an African American quarterback. To not only be the first in Badger Football History but the first in the History of the Big Ten.

SIDNEY WILLIAMS
22
WISCONSIN BADGERS

Sidney William's song "Aint No Stoppin Me" by Shelton Benjamin. *"Ain't no stoppin me now! Going for it all. Just trying to be the best. See me breakin out. Nothing more, nothing less. Ain't no stoppin me now."*

"First"

Some people may not enjoy being described as "First" at something. I get it, I have always been introduced at the first quarterback in the history of St. John's Jesuit High School when I speak somewhere. At First it bothered me for many years because I felt that I had accomplished a myriad of other things that were much more important than being the first quarterback in the history of St. John's Jesuit. But I started to understand what being "First" really stands for, what it really means. It meant you were a trailblazer; it means you helped to make the path a little easier for the people that followed you. So, in retrospect, with many years in the rear-view mirror, being "First" in most endeavors is a true honor. Again, you are helping others to succeed who have come after you.

So, in "Black in the Pocket" when we write about the First Black quarterback at a particular college or the first Black quarterback on a professional team in the CFL or the NFL, to me it is the ultimate compliment because it is never easy being "First," that position is always fraught with issues and problems. But "First" is an honor!

They Don't Know

All the so-called NFL scouts and coaches and owners all think they have a clear eye in picking quarterback talent. That talent mostly White until the last ten years, but also including Black, Hispanics, Asians, it does not matter the experts are wrong the good majority of the time on what will make a successful pro quarterback. There were so many top quarterback picks that just weren't good picks like the following:

Charlie Fry was a round 3 draft pick by Cleveland. He could not play well consistently, great at Akron but not in Cleveland.

Quincy Carter, a round 2 draft pick by Dallas was a great athlete but not consistent. He had some wonderful NFL games but not enough.

Danny Wuerffel a round 4 pick by the New Orleans Saints, had no arm strength. He was very smart, great mind but not enough arm for the NFL.

Rob Johnson was a round 4 pick by Buffalo. A mediocre player in Jacksonville and as a pro showed signs of brilliance but could not do it consistently.

John Beck, a round 2 pick by Miami. Just not an NFL quarterback, he was a good college quarterback, but his skill set was not made for the NFL.

Browning Nagle was a round 2 pick by the New York Jets but made no impact at quarterback, again a very good college player but just did not work out in the NFL.

Mike Elkins, a round 2 pick by the Kansas City Chiefs never found a place in the NFL at quarterback. A good college player that never got comfortable in the NFL.

Jason Campbell was a round 1 pick by the Washington Redskins. Jason had too many injuries, too many turnovers and could not stay healthy in the NFL.

Rex Grossman was a round 1 pick by the Chicago Bears. He forced too many passes in the NFL, too many interceptions. Great College player, poor pro player.

Patrick Ramsey another round 1 pick by the Redskins could never get past being a back-up quarterback. He was very good as a college quarterback and leader, just not a good fit in the NFL.

Ty Detmer a round 9 pick by Green Bay, did not have enough arm strength. A good person, good leader, great college career but could not stretch the field in the NFL.

Gino Torretta, a round 7 pick by Minnesota. He did not see the field well but was a good college quarterback player, less than average pro player.

Eric Crouch, a round 3 pick by St. Louis. Eric was an excellent college athlete but coming from Nebraska did not come from a pro system.

Gary Beban was a round 2 pick by Washington. Gary was a remarkable college quarterback that never got a chance in the NFL. Coach George Allen did not play rookies, totally unfair to Beban.

John Huarte a round 2 pick by the New York Jets. Huarte was a solid quarterback from Notre Dame, but he was never going to beat out Joe Namath.

Mark Malone was around 1 draft pick by the Steelers. He was just average at quarterback in the Pros' that showed flashes of brilliance but could not be consistent.

Kerry Collins was a round 1 draft pick by Carolina. Kerry was a good college quarterback but had too many turnovers in the NFL, and not a great passing motion.

Brady Quinn was a round 1 draft pick by the Browns. Brady did not have the arm talent, very good at Notre Dame, but not an NFL arm.

Tony Eason a round 1 draft pick by the Patriots. He could not perform at the level he did in college, in the NFL.

Pat Sullivan was a round 2 draft pick by Atlanta. He was incredible in college but had no touch on the ball, every pass was a fastball.

Kyle Boller, a round 1 draft pick by the Baltimore Ravens, had trouble reading NFL defenses.

Jeff George, a round 1 pick by the Colts, had an incredible arm but not the right mental approach to succeed in the NFL.

Terry Baker was a round 1 pick by Los Angeles. He was a fantastic college quarterback, a real standout that did not get a fair opportunity. He could throw with either hand and was also a fantastic basketball player. He played in the Final Four.

Steve Spurrier, drafted by San Francisco in round 1. An incredible college quarterback but his skills did not translate in the NFL. He became a fantastic coach.

Jack Thompson was drafted in the 1st round by the Bengals. He was a remarkable college quarterback and just did not get the right opportunity in the NFL.

Todd Blackledge, a round 1 pick by Kansas City did not have a fluid passing motion, a stepper and thrower who did not work out in the NFL.

David Carr was picked by Houston in round 1 of the draft. He was a great college quarterback that got hit too many times in the NFL which hurt his development.

Joey Harrington, a round 1 pick in the draft by the Detroit Lions. He just did not have a true feel for the Pro passing game.

Rich Campbell was drafted in the 1st round by the Green Bay Packers. He was a great college passer but never started a single game in the NFL.

David Klingler, picked by the Bengals in round 1 of the draft. He was a great thrower in college but running the run and shoot offense in college hurt him in the Pro game.

Rick Mirer was drafted in round 1 by Seattle. He did not have a fluid passing motion and had a tough time reading defenses and finding open receivers in the NFL but was an outstanding Qb in College at Notre Dame.

Andre Ware was a round 1 draft pick by the Detroit Lions. He played the run and shoot offense in Houston in College to great success but had a total lack of training for the Pro passing game.

Tim Couch was selected in round 1 by the Cleveland Browns. Couch was a good short thrower but had difficulty going deep and stretching the field. He was successful as a college quarterback.

Akili Smith was drafted in the 1st round by Cincinnati. He had a skill set that made him successful in college but not a good fit in the NFL.

Art Schlichter was drafted in round one by the Colts. His personal problems took his game away from him in the NFL. He was an outstanding quarterback in college.

Heath Shuler was drafted in the 1st round by Washington. He was a highly successful quarterback at Tennessee but had real trouble understanding the professional quarterback position and the diverse types of passes you had to throw.

JaMarcus Russell was drafted in round 1 by the Los Angeles Raiders. He had a good college career, but his work ethic, weight and lack of focus ended any chance to succeed in the NFL.

Ryan Leaf was drafted by San Diego in round 1. He was an outstanding quarterback in college, but immaturity, personal issues and temperament problems stopped him from having a career of not in the NFL.

All these top round draft picks in the NFL, at the quarterback position, just did not work out for a myriad of reasons. Some were great in college, yet their skill set did not translate in the NFL. The NFL is a vastly different game from college from the quarterback position. It moves so much faster and all the athletes on the field are outstanding. Speed is everywhere on the field. Receivers in the NFL are not open like they are in college. Many times, you have to throw them open, many times you have to throw to spots and many times you must anticipate the throw, throw the ball well before the break of the receiver. And the people on Defense that are rushing you from the pocket are bigger, stronger, and faster than you have ever seen in college.

In the NFL from the quarterback position, because of the immense size of the offensive lines and defensive line, men 6'5", 6'6" or 6'7" in height, you have to find windows to be able to throw the football. In the NFL game you have to learn to get the ball in and out of your hands very quickly.

It is incredible how many times head coaches and scouts and owners make the most important decisions in the NFL, and that is at the quarterback position and yet from the 1960's to modern day 2023, they are only correct about 50% of the time, about as correct as your local weatherman.

So, these experts say they know White, Black, Hispanic, or Asian at the quarterback position in the NFL but in reality, they do not have a clue. They would have as much luck if they just put the college quarterback prospects on a dart board and threw darts. Why do so many of these genuinely great college quarterbacks fail, regardless of color? They were outstanding in college and talented enough to be a top draft pick. They all had remarkable success in college, but when they get that dart board pick in the NFL why does it not work at least 50% of the time? All these top round NFL draft picks at the quarterback position were tremendously talented, so what goes wrong? Why does the NFL quarterback system not work? First, I think the most difficult thing to do in all of sports is to drop back in the pocket and try to find someone open in the NFL. But major fail reasons at the quarterback position in the NFL are twofold. A bad quarterback system, putting a quarterback in a system that does not fit his strength and bad coaching from the quarterback position, no position in the NFL needs more coaching or mentoring, more guidance, more encouragement than the quarterback position.

Even in the NFL you need to work on the quarterback fundamentals, their feet on the drop back, their steps per route, their passing motion, their passing arc, working quick feet to set-up in the pocket or the gun and short fluid passing motion that allow you to get the ball out of your hands quickly, yet with pace, timing and accuracy. Lastly a quarterback in the NFL needs to be inserted into games when they are ready, when they have a chance to be successful, not put into a Pro game because they were a top round draft pick and paid a lot of money.

The quarterback position, at any level, whether it is high school, college or Pro is one of development and creating success for the quarterback which breeds confidence, because without confidence you cannot play in the NFL at the quarterback position. So, when these NFL experts, coaches and scouts or TV talking heads with motor oil in their hair like Mel Kiper, tell you a particular college quarterback will be great in the NFL, run for the hills; because "they don't know."

46

First Black Quarterback at Northwestern

Kain Colter played football for the Northwestern Wildcats, played two positions, quarterback and wide receiver. Colter is also a co-founder of the College Athletes Players Association or CAPA, which is a labor organization established to assert college athletes' status as employees with the right to collectively bargain for basic protections.

As a true freshman at Northwestern Colter made his first college start for the Wildcats as a slotback in the 2011 Ticket City Bowl. As a sophomore Colter got to start at quarterback against Boston College, he led the Wildcats to a 24-17 victory. Colter's career passing numbers at Northwestern are 233 completions in 322 attempts for 2,166 yards and 18 touchdowns.

Colter was not drafted in the NFL but signed a deal with the Vikings as a free agent. He made the practice squad. Colter also spent time with the Los Angeles Rams and the Buffalo Bills on their practice squads. Colter at Northwestern was a three-time academic All American and a leader for four years and co-captain of the Wildcat Football Team plus being the first Black quarterback in the history of Northwestern University.

KAIN COLTER

2

NORTHWESTERN UNIVERSITY

Kain Colter's song by Joe South "Walk a Mile in My Shoes." *"If I could be you, if you could be me for just one hour, if we could find a way to get inside each other's mind. If you could see you through my eyes instead of your ego, I believe you'd be surprised to see you have been blind.*

Sandy Stevens
Minnesota

47

Sandy Stephen arrived on campus at the University of Minnesota in 1958. As a first-year student, he was ineligible to compete in the football program his first year on campus. In 1959 he shared time as a quarterback of the Minnesota Gopher Football Team and became Minnesota's first Black quarterback in the history of the program. He also helped to lead Minnesota to a National Title, leading the Maroon and Gold to an 8-2 record. Sandy Stephens also led the team to its first and only Rose Bowl victory in 1962. Stephens was also an All American at Minnesota. One of Sandy's teammates, Judge Dickson, said that Sandy was solely responsible for bringing the Minnesota team together and making all the players understand that Minnesota could come together with a Black quarterback and win.

Sandy had faith; he knew how to lead others. He used to keep a picture of the Rose Bowl in his room. He told all his teammates that someday the Gophers would be in the Rose Bowl. Some laughed, the ones that listened to Sandy eventually made it to the Rose Bowl. Sandy Stevens the Gopher's quarterback won a Rose Bowl and Sandy was named MVP and was the first Black quarterback to win a Rose Bowl.

Sandy was drafted in the first round of the AFL by the New York Titans, but they wanted to make him a wide receiver, so he left.

SANDY STEVENS
15
UNIVERSITY OF MINNESOTA

Sandy's song is "Photograph" by Ringo Starr. *"Everytime I see your face it reminds me of the places we used to go but all I've got is a photograph and I realize you're not coming back anymore"*

Sandy Stevens picture in his college room with his visualization got him and his Minnesota Football Teammates to the Rose Bowl. Have a goal, put a picture up like Sandy Stevens did!

What Needed to Happen

What needed to happen in college and pro football for Black players to receive the fair opportunities that they deserved? I think like a CEO in any organization, the attitudes the atmosphere all stems from the CEO leadership at the top. The head football coach in college or the NFL is the CEO of the football organization. The head coach in football at a college or in the Pro's is a monarch, a ruler over his kingdom. Head coaches of football teams tend not to have any democratic principles in running their football program. One man, one rule, sure they let players choose captains or talk to them about uniform choices, but make no mistake a head football coach, whether it be in high school, college or the Pro's is truly a dictator. Giving you a practical example in high school I played for the same head coach for four years at the quarterback position. In four years, I checked off on a play and ran something else one time. He pulled me out of the game immediately and made me go sit in the band bus for the entire second half of the game. I sat in the bus with the tuba players. Do not kid yourself, head football coaches at any level are absolute rulers. They set the tempo and the climate and environment on any football organization.

In the 1960's, 1970's and into the 1980's it was very apparent that the head college football coaches in the North and the Midwest were much more open to giving Black players their rightful opportunities with football scholarships, to be able to play and compete and receive an excellent education. Whereas in the South some head coaches were very reticent to do what was right as far as playing Black players and helping them to get a football scholarship to be able to get a quality education.

Why did so many Southern coaches put their heads in the sand and ignore the racial component to their football team? So, the salient point is why so many coaches in the South in the 1960's, 1970's and 1980's did not do the right thing as far as race is concerned on their football team.

The easy answer is the political environment in the Southern states and in the United States where discrimination was rampant. Many of these head football coaches, these CEOs did not want to upset people. But they were wrong, they were leaders of young men they had an obligation to be a leader, to be a role model. Many people say that football builds character, which I am sure is partially true, but I truly feel what football does is it reveals character.

The head football coaches in the South especially in the 60's and 70's that did not aggressively integrate their teams, failed to be a true leaders. Real leadership is when things are not easy but you chose to stand up and do the right thing. When you are going to face adversity or very harsh criticism. What do you do? Do you ignore the criticism, not let the adversity affect you? True leadership is doing the right thing when it is really a difficult thing to do. Anyone can lead when things are easy but when things are very difficult that's where real leadership occurs. And just ask yourself this question, what might have happened in our society if football coaches in the South in the 1960's and 1970's did the right thing, did the hard thing in a difficult George Wallacesque environment and totally integrated their teams in the 1960's and 1970's. Football coaches are held in high esteem in our society and if more of the Southern Coaches had done the right thing when they had the opportunity, we would all have been better off. And America would have been much further ahead in race relations. As Mark Twain said, "You're never wrong doing the right thing."

George Taliaferro
Indiana

49

George Taliaferro would play many positions at the University of Indiana from 1945 to 1948. George played quarterback, half back, defensive back and kicker. But from the standpoint of Indiana Football History, he was the first Black quarterback in the history of the school. George faced many forms of racism on the Indiana Campus from 1945 to 1948. George had to deal with being barred from living in dormitories and sometimes impolite treatment from his teammates just because he was Black.

George was an All American at Indiana University and helped to lead his teammates to an undefeated season in the Big Ten. The only one Indiana has ever had. He also led the Big Ten in rushing, the first time an African American had ever done that in the Big Ten. George ran for 719 yards on 156 carries in 1945, which were league leading stats. Taliaferro was especially important in helping to break the color barrier. George Taliaferro played two years before Jackie Robinson suited up with the Dodgers. George was drafted by the Chicago Bears in the 13th round of the 1949 NFL Draft, but he decided to play for the LA Dons of the All-American Football Conference.

George Taliaferro became the first African American to be drafted in the NFL. George eventually moved back to play in the NFL and had the following NFL Stats, rushing touchdowns 15, rushing yards 2,266, carries 498, receptions 95, and receiving yards 1,300.

In his career George played for the LA Dons in 1949, The New York Yanks 1950-1951, the Dallas Texans in 1952, Baltimore Colts 1953-1954 and the Philadelphia Eagles in 1955. He was a three-time Pro Bowl pick in the NFL. In College, First Team All American and two-time First Team All-Big Ten.

When George retired from football, he became a Big Brother and Big Sister volunteer. He also got his master's degree in social work. Then he became a special assistant to the President of Indiana University. His wife Viola entered Indiana Law School when she graduated and worked in law until she was eventually appointed to a Judge position. George Taliaferro and his incredibly talented wife were true difference makers in life and especially at Indiana University, and remarkable role models for the Hoosier student body.

GEORGE TALIAFERRO
20
INDIANA UNIVERSITY

George's song is "For the First Time" by Darius Rucker. *"When was the last time you did something for the first time? Yeah, let yourself go follow that feeling, maybe something new is what you're needing."*

Condredge Holloway
"The Artful Dodger"

Condredge Holloway was the first Black quarterback in the history of the University of Tennessee as well as the first Black quarterback in the history of the Southeast Conference in 1972. In three years as a starter at Tennessee he led the Volunteers (Vols) to the 1972 Astro Bluebonnet Bowl, the 1973 Gator Bowl and the 1974 Liberty Bowl.

Condredge was the University of Tennessee's first Black Baseball player. Baseball was actually his favorite sport. While at Tennessee, Condredge maintained a 351 average and collected 145 hits with 62 RBI's.

After 13 seasons as a quarterback in the Canadian Football League he returned to the University of Tennessee to work. The University of Tennessee retired his number 1 baseball jersey in 2015. Condredge was assistant athletic director for student-athlete relations and lettermen when he retired in 2019.

Condredge is the only University of Tennessee student Athlete named to the All-Century Squads in Baseball and Football. Holloway's record as a starting quarterback at Tennessee was 23-9-2. His total offense was 4,068 yards, he completed 238 passes in 407 attempts, and he had 18 touchdown passes. Condredge threw for 3,102 yards. He also rushed for 966 yards on 351 attempts. He also had 9 rushing touchdowns.

In 1975 Holloway was drafted by the New England Patriots in the 12th round as a defensive back. He was a great quarterback not a defensive back. So, Holloway did what Chuck Ealey did before him and said no to the NFL and a position change and yes to the Canadian Football League. Holloway started playing for the Ottawa Rough Riders in 1975 and later moved to the Toronto Argonauts where he became the Canadian Football League's most outstanding player in 1982 and guiding the Argos to a Grey Cup Championship. The following season it was Toronto's first title in 31 years. Holloway finished his career with the BC Lions and was inducted into the Canadian Football Hall of Fame in 1999. After Football Holloway went on to become assistant athletic director at the University of Tennessee.

One of the genuinely great basketball players at the University of Tennessee, Terry Crosby, who knew Condredge Holloway, said of the quarterback, "he was a great leader, tough as nails, so very smart and always poised in the pocket. He was an incredible personality, everyone liked him, and he was very coachable."

The problem with Condredge Holloway was not Condredge Holloway but with the NFL. He should have been given an opportunity to prove that what he did at the University of Tennessee he could do in the NFL. He never got the chance because of the short-sighted views of NFL Coaches and owners in the 1970's. They needed to look at what a great all-around athlete and leader Condredge Holloway was.

He was drafted fourth by the Montreal Expos to play baseball. He was offered football scholarships, Bear Bryant offered him one at Alabama, but again the same old caveat that so many great Black quarterbacks had to deal with. Bryant told Condredge that he could never play quarterback at Alabama. But he could play another position. What a shame Bryant did not have the commitment to fairness and the courage to give Holloway a chance. But to his credit Coach Battle at Tennessee told Holloway that he could play quarterback at Tennessee. At that time there was no Black quarterback in the SEC, Holloway would be the first. He would be the trailblazer and trailblazer he truly was. Orange No. 7 torched his way through the Southeast Conference. He could run and throw and was very difficult to tackle hence his nickname, that was one of the best in all of college football, "The Artful Dodger." And to Bill Battle's continued credit, Battle said, "I never thought of Condredge Holloway as anything but a quarterback" and that is the way that it should be!

CONDREDGE HOLLOWAY
7
TENNESSEE

The song I picked for Condredge was "It's so Hard to Hold On" by Trampled by Turtles. *"It's so hard, it's so hard to hold on, it's so hard, it's so hard to hold on"*

It was very difficult to hang on to Condredge Holloway, he was harder to hold than a basket of leaves on a windy day!

Left to Soon
Omar Jacobs

Omar Jacobs played college football at Bowling Green University. He was drafted by the Pittsburgh Steelers in the fifth round of the NFL Draft in 2006. In 2004 he set a record for the best touchdown to interception in NCAA Division 1 College Football. He was expected to contend for the Heisman Trophy his junior year but hurt his non-throwing shoulder, which hurt his ability to throw. Omar then decided to skip his senior year at BGSU and go into the NFL Draft. Omar left Bowling Green as the all-time leader in touchdown passes at 71 and third in career passing yards with 6,938 yards. He was also first team All MAC and MAC offensive player of the year. After being selected in the fifth round by the Pittsburgh Steelers at the end of his pre-season play, he was sent to the practice squad. In the following training camp with the Pittsburgh Steelers, he was cut from the team. In 2006 Omar Jacobs was signed by the Philadelphia Eagles then cut in 2007. Then he was signed by the Kansas City Chiefs. Omar also played for many years in the Arena Football League.

If Jacobs had stayed one more year with a strong, solid senior season he could have been a first-round draft pick at quarterback in the NFL. I think that he was given bad advice that if he left as a junior, he would be a first-round draft choice. That was not to be. Omar Jacobs made a mistake. He needed one more strong senior season to prove his passing mechanics and improve his feet throwing from the pocket. If he had done that, everything could have been different.

As they say in life or any profession "Timing is Everything" especially when you are talking about the quarterback position.

OMAR JACOBS
4
BOWLING GREEN UNIVERSITY

Omar's song is "Left to Soon" by Mick Kolassa. *"I just wasn't ready, it all came to fast. I never dreamed that yesterday would be the last!"*

52

Cradle of Quarterbacks at the University of Toledo

There must be something in the water from the Ottawa River that runs through the University of Toledo because Toledo produces quarterbacks at an alarming rate. Their history of outstanding quarterbacks is truly a remarkable story.

The number one University of Toledo quarterback is Chuck Ealey. Ealey was a 1971 first team All American. He was a three-time first team All MAC quarterback. Ealey led the Toledo Rockets to three consecutive undefeated seasons going 35-0 as a starting quarterback. He never lost a game as a starting quarterback in high school or high college. He finished eighth in the voting for the Heisman Trophy in 1971. He then went to Canada and won the Grey Cup his first season in the Canadian Football League.

The next University of Toledo Rocket quarterback was Bruce Gradkowski. He was first team All-Mac and an honorable mention All American. Gradkowski is the Rockets career leader in passing yards at 9,225, passing completions 766 and touchdown passes at 85. Gradkowski led the University of Toledo to a MAC Championship. He also played ten seasons in the NFL.

The next great quarterback at the University of Toledo was Gene Swick from 1973-1975. In 1975 Swick was named first team All

American and tenth in the Heisman balloting in 1975. Swick was three-time first team Mac and had a tryout with the Cleveland Browns.

Next up for the Rockets at quarterback was John Schneider. He was two-time All Mac. He set 17 University of Toledo passing records. He also led the University of Toledo to a share of its first Mac Crown. Schnieder then went on to play quarterback in the Canadian Football League.

The next great quarterback at the University of Toledo was Lee Pete from 1946 to 1949. Pete was a first team All Ohio pick in 1947. Pete finished his career at the University of Toledo with 23 touchdown passes which was a school record at that time. He had one of the best arms in the country. He could throw the ball 70 yards in the air. Lee Pete had tryouts with the Detroit Lions and Green Bay Packers.

The next University of Toledo Rocket quarterback in the pocket was Ryan Huzjak 1993-1996. He was a two time All Mac player and was the last Rocket quarterback to lead an undefeated team.

The current great UT Rocket quarterback is Dequan Finn 2022-2023. Dequan's 1277 career rushing yards ranks as second all-time at Toledo among quarterbacks with 18 rushing touchdowns. In 2022 he was the second team all Mac quarterback passing for 2,269 yards and 23 touchdowns and led Toledo to a Mac Championship.

The next particularly important quarterback for the University of Toledo was Steve Jones. He was the first Black starting quarterback in the history of the University of Toledo. His starting year was 1968. He led the Rockets to a winning record of 5-4. His career stats were 108 completions with 278 attempts. His passing yardage in 1968 was 1309 yards. But being the first African American quarterback to start for the Toledo Rockets, he opened the door for Chuck Ealey the next year, who went on to win 35 games in a row. Steve Jones was an exceptionally good runner and rushed for over 1000 yards from the quarterback position in his career, that is extremely difficult to do.

There was one other potential quarterback star at the University of Toledo, but he did not play quarterback, he played halfback for the Toledo Rockets, his name was Emlen Tunnell, and he played in 1942. He unfortunately got hurt trying to make a tackle against Marshall. His neck was broken. He recovered to help lead the Rocket Men's Basketball Team to the finals in 1943 in the National Invitation Tournament. Tunnell's neck injury resulted in his being rejected by the army and navy during WWII. But Emlen then enlisted in the United States Coast Guard. He wanted to do his part. From August 1943 to July 1944, he served on the USS Etamin. In April 1944, the Etamin was struck by a torpedo dropped from a Japanese airplane. Emlen saved a fellow crew member who was set on fire because of the blast. He beat out the flames with his bare hands and even though his hands were burned he carried his shipmate to safety. In the fall of 1944 Tunnell played halfback for the San Francisco Coast Pilots Football Team and he threw two touchdowns totaling 22 yards to win the championship. In March of 1946 Tunnell again saved a shipmate who fell off the USS Tampa. Emlen jumped in the 32-degree water and again saved his shipmate. The Coast Guard named a ship after Emlen in 2017, the USCGC Emlen Tunnell. Emlen was honorably discharged from the Coast Guard in April 1946. He enrolled at the University of Iowa in 1946. In 1946 he led the Iowa team in passing with 28 completions and rushed for 333 yards.

On July 24, 1948, Tunnell signed with the New York Giants. He became the first African American football player to play with the New York Giants. Emlen had to hitchhike to his try-out with the Giants. Emlin Tunnell was known as one of the best pass defenders and punt returners in the NFL. In 1952 he was selected for the first team All Pro. Tunnell remained with the Giants for 11 years, 1948 to 1958. He was selected All Pro six times. He played in eight Pro Bowls. He set a Giants record that still stands today, 74 interceptions for 1,240 yards. After the 1958 Giants Football Season, Vince Lombardi left as an assistant to become the head coach of the Green Bay Packers and he took Emlen Tunnell with him, that is how much Lombardi thought of Emlen Tunnell. In February of 1967 Emlen Tunnell was the first African American to go into the Pro Football Hall of Fame. He was the first player that only played defense to get into the Pro Football Hall of Fame. He was also ranked the second greatest player to ever play for the New York Giants.

EMLEN TUNNELL

45

NEW YORK GIANTS

Emlen's song is "American Soldier" by Toby Keith. *"You can bet I stand ready when the wolf growls at the door, Hey, I'm solid, hey I'm steady, hey I'm true down to my core and I will always do my duty no matter what the price. I've counted up the cost, I know the sacrifice. Oh, and I don't want to die for you but if dying's asked of me I'll bear that cross with honor."*

First African American Quarterback at the University of Texas

53

Donnie Little was the quarterback of the Texas Longhorns from 1978 to 1980 and in 1978 was the first Black Quarterback to play for the University of Texas. Donnie Little is credited with opening doors for future Black quarterbacks to play at the University of Texas. After being heavily recruited and choosing Texas over Oklahoma, Little played for Texas from 1978 to 1981. In 1979 Little's sophomore season at Texas. He started the first nine games at quarterback and Texas went 8-1 and helped to lead Texas to a number 6 ranking in the country even making it to number one in the country at one point. In 1980 Little was again the starting quarterback for Texas. He set a school record for most passing yards against Rice at 306. Even with the success that Little had as a quarterback for Texas in the spring of 1981 he asked to be switched to wide receiver because he knew he would not get much of a chance to play quarterback in the NFL, given the history of how they treated Black quarterbacks. That year Donnie became the leading receiver for Texas that season.

Over his career Little played in 29 games and led the team in total offense in 1979 and 1980. He passed for 2,067 yards and had 338 yards receiving and rushed for 1,334 yards in his career at Texas. His record as starting quarterback was 15-5 and Donnie Little is listed as one of the all- time top ten quarterbacks in the history of the University of Texas.

Donnie was not selected in the NFL draft. He was then signed by the Atlanta Falcons but cut before the season started. Donnie then went to the Canadian Football League and played for the Ottawa Rough Riders where he was a quarterback, wide receiver, punt returner and kick-off returner. Donnie was considered by many to be the best athlete on the team. He then suffered a severe knee injury and his football career was over.

Then Donnie tried to play professional baseball but that did not work out. He then spent 24 years working for the University of Texas as a fundraiser. Donnie was an incredibly gifted athlete and a talented quarterback that did not ever get a shot at taking one snap at quarterback in the NFL. This was the mindset that so many coaches and owners had in the NFL in the early 1980's, again move the talented Black athlete to another position.

DONNIE LITTLE
1
TEXAS

Donnie's song "Changes" by David Bowie. "Ch-ch-ch changes, turn and face the strange ch-ch-changes. Don't want to be a riches man ch-ch-changes. Turn and face the strange ch-ch-changes, Theres gonna have to be a different man, time may change me, but I can't change time."

NFL's Shameful History in the 50's, 60's, 70's and 80's

The NFL history in the 1950's, 1960's, 1970's and into the 1980's in regard to giving African American players and quarterbacks their equal and fair opportunity in the NFL was shameful. Why is this? Well Common sense tells us that the people for the most part making decisions in the NFL are White. There are 32 teams in the NFL for the 2024 NFL Football Season with six African American Head Coaches. Only 7 of the 32 owners are minorities. However none of them are Black, for that matter there has never been a Black Owner in the 104 year history. In 2024 53% of the NFL Players are Black and around 36% were Black Assistant Coaches. With those stats how in the world can there be just 6 Black Head Coaches going into the 2024 season. The NFL has not had an African American Owner in 104 years.

Progress is being made on the playing field. For the first time in the history of the NFL two Black Quarterbacks started in the Super Bowl. And there are currently 14 starting African American Qb's in the NFL, that is moving the needle forward, this is providing opportunities. But the NFL desperately needs to do better as far as minority ownership and minority head coaches. The Rooney Rule, though well intended, has been a titanic failure and it needs to be rethought. Old White guys making decisions on starting quarterbacks in the NFL or hiring head coaches in the NFL or allowing a minority to own a team has never been a good thing. It has never produced fair and equitable thinking. It is a very closed circle that old White guys like to exclude minorities and women and not allow them fair and equal access to jobs. (OWG) Old White Guys have a shameful history of hiring in the NFL.

Minnesota's Most Famous Quarterback

Tony Dungy received a bachelor's degree in business administration from the University of Minnesota in 1978. He played quarterback for the Gophers from 1973-1976. Dungy, when he retired from the University of Minnesota held many records. He finished as the school leader in pass attempts, completions, passing yardage and touchdown passes. Dungy was also the Gophers most valuable player in 1975 and in 1976. In 1977 he was awarded the Big Ten Medal of Honor for academic excellence.

In spite of all of those records and remarkable accomplishments at the University of Minnesota Dungy did not get drafted to play quarterback in the NFL. Tony Dungy was so very bright that he knew he could play quarterback in the NFL. But when Pittsburg signed him as a free agent, they made him switch to defensive back. Tony played three seasons in the NFL. He also won a Super Bowl with the Pittsburg Steelers. Dungy said he did not feel that back in his day the NFL did not look at "out of the box quarterbacks" quarterbacks that can really move around and scramble and run, not just sit in the pocket, and try to throw the ball away and avoid sacks. Today the "out of the box" quarterback as Dungy calls them are an NFL reality. That is thriving visa vie Patrick Mahomes and Jalen Hurts. The first two African American quarterbacks to start in a Super Bowl in last year's big game.

Tony Dungy went on to become one of the best head coaches in the NFL at Tampa Bay where he got his team to the Super Bowl and with the Baltimore Colts Dungy guided the Colts in 2006 to an AFC South Title then beat New England 38-34 in the AFC Championship game. Then in Super Bowl XLI Dungy and his Indianapolis Colts defeated the Chicago Bears 29-17 to win Super Bowl XLI.

He became the first African American Head Coach to win a Super Bowl. That should have opened the floodgates in the NFL for more African American Head Coaches, it did not. Why not? You still have to look at a reoccurring theme in the NFL (OWG). Old White guys controlled the league and still do today. I think what was done is the coaching game was stacked against the Black coach to become a head coach in the NFL. They, the hiring bosses of the NFL, pushed and funneled Black assistant coaches into defensive coordinator positions when the league from the 1970's to present time was about offense and quarterbacks. So, if you were an offensive coordinator in the NFL, you had a much better opportunity to be a head coach in the NFL. I think that is still going on today with just 6 Black Head Coaches starting for the 2024 season, with 32 teams and more than half the players in the NFL being Black, that math does not work. But no system of employment, no matter how flawed, could keep Tony Dungy down. He was a great NFL player, Super Head Coach, Pro Football Hall of Famer and TV star analyst for Pro Football. Tony has had an incredible career but somewhere sometimes in the back of his mind he has to have that occasional thought of "I could have been a standout QB in the NFL if I was given my rightful opportunity to take that snap, drop back, find an open receiver down field and deliver the ball or if nothing was there take off and run. Tony Dungy has to think in the very deep recesses of his mind, "that could have been me in the pocket."

TONY DUNGY
9
MINNESOTA UNIVERSITY GOPHERS

Tony's song would be by Yvonne air, *"It Should Have Been Me." "It should have been me. You know that it should have been me, You know it should have been me."*

Toledo Football Footnote to Tony Dungy – for almost 50 years the University of Toledo's Chuck Ealey, Number 16, was denied entrance into the College Football Hall of Fame, but that ended when Tony Dungy called the Hall of Fame and very strongly suggested Ealey belongs. Ealey never lost a college football game. Chuck Ealey is now in the College Football Hall of Fame. Thank you, Tony Dungy!

56

Beware of the Pompadour

Mel Kiper on ESPN is part of the problem with as Tony Dungy calls them out of the box quarterbacks getting a fair shot in the NFL. Many of those quarterbacks through the years were African American. Kiper is smart, he does his homework and is very analytical. But I bet anything you want that Mel never played a down of football. Ok, I had to look it up. He never played any football or coached football anywhere. He was a JV pitcher in high school for a season or so. I say in the title beware the pompadour, Mel has more grease in his hair than most fast-food fryers. You could light a blue tip match off his American Graffiti haircut.

Kiper is very bright and very entrepreneurial. He had a futuristic view of the NFL. He saw a need and delivered it. The hunger that fans had for the NFL draft information was insatiable. One of the problems with Mel is that he has no accountability. He is wrong a lot. But often ESPN does not go back and rate Mel's picks, how many were right and how many were wrong. They do not do that for a reason. Because Kiper misses a lot. ESPN does not want to draw attention to Mel's misses. All ESPN cares about is that people like Joe Hotdog in his basement spending endless hours watching the NFL draft believe that Kiper must know what he is talking about, or he would not be on TV. ESPN could care less about Mel's correctness. It is about ratings, style and no substance. Mel Kiper is a circus barker standing outside the tent and enticing ESPN

162

viewers in. He is incorrect more than a very mediocre weatherman from El Segundo. Mel would be better served being a waiter at a mid-level Manhattan restaurant then he is able to tell you who the next great NFL quarterback will be.

His ability to judge top NFL quarterback talent is really suspect. Case in point, he did not think Russell Wilson would be great in the NFL. He thought Andre Ware was a first-round quarterback pick. Mel said Dan McGuire was an equal talent to Brett Favre. Mel also thought Rick Mier and Brady Quinn would be very good NFL quarterbacks. Mel said that DeMarcus Russell was an equal talent to John Elway. Mel also felt that Johnny Football aka Johnny Manziel would be a talent in the NFL comparable to Fran Tarkenton.

Mel, you need to get a new haircut, maybe something like Larry Fine or Moe Howard one of the Three Stooges or go with the Curly Howard look and get all that greasy kids' stuff out of your hair and out of your eyes and maybe you could see more clearly what a real NFL quarterback looks like.

57

Ole Miss First Black Starting Quarterback

Former Ole Miss Football player Roy Coleman was a three-year lettered athlete from 1977 to 1979. He passed away in Memphis on February 5, 2013. at the age of 54. Roy was the first Black starting quarterback in the history of Ole Miss Football. Coleman was an integral part of the 1977 Mississippi Team that knocked off eventual national champion Notre Dame in Jackson Mississippi. He spent most of his time as a starting flanker his sophomore season in 1977 and had a 52 yard catch in that 20-13 huge win over the Irish on September 17, 1977. Roy started six games as quarterback for Mississippi his junior year and he passed for 448 yards and rushed for 162 yards and three scores.

As a senior Roy decided to give baseball a try and made the Rebel team as a pitcher. Roy went on to earn a bachelor's degree from the University of Mississippi and then went on to become a firefighter. Roy had three daughters and a son.

Roy Coleman's passing numbers at Ole Miss were as follows: 47 out 115 for 583 yards and one touchdown.

ROY COLEMAN
12
MISSISSIPPI UNIVERSITY

Roy's song is by Foreigner, "It Feels like the First Time." "It feels like the first time, feels like the very first time, it feels like the very first time"

58

Blackway Joe/ Broadway Joe

The First Black quarterback in the History of the NFL was not Black. The most universally accepted rookie quarterback in the history of Pro Football in the early 1960's was Joe William Namath better known as Broadway Joe or Joe Willie.

Joe Namath came from the integrated neighborhoods of Beaver Falls, Pennsylvania. Many of his best friends growing up were African American. All his sports teams were integrated in high school. Joe Namath did not see color. When he went to segregated Alabama to play football, he put a picture of one of his high school friends in his dorm room and it was an African American young lady. Namath was verbally accosted by his teammates on an all-white Alabama Football Team. And when Namath was drafted number one by the New York Jets in 1965, the Jets were a team that had a separate side to the team as far as Black Players and White Players were concerned. Joe Willie Namath changed all that by his friendly style and accepting ways. He never saw color; they were just teammates.

So many African American Pro Football players really enjoyed Joe's style of play on and off the field. His clothes, his car, his White shoes, and his long hair. Namath thumbed his nose at the establishment that was the NFL. He was a Rebel and a non-conformist. He stood-up against authority, stood up against the old guard in Pro Football that said this is how you do things, because this is always how things were done. That was never true for Joe Namath and the Black athletes in Pro Football had the utmost respect for him. They saw Joe as one of them against the system, that again was run by old white guys. It was a Black offensive lineman for the Jets that gave Namath his famous nickname, "Broadway Joe." Sherman Plunkett coined that name that has stuck with Namath even today. Through the 13 years of Namath's professional career many of the Black defensive players whose job it was to kill the quarterback tried very carefully never to hit Namath unfairly. He represented so much to the African American players in Pro Football and still does today.

JOE "WILLIE" NAMATH
12
NEW YORK JETS

Joe's song by Three Dog Night, "Black and White." "The world is Black, the world is White, It turns by day and then by night. A child is Black, a child is White, together they grow to see the light, to see the light."

The Kiper Conundrum with Quarterbacks

The problem with Mel Kiper trying to tell you who is going to be a good quarterback in the NFL is two-fold. Mel never played football at any level and never coached at any level. So Kiper very smartly figured out that he personally does not know anything about the quarterback position so having a very keen analytical mind he decided to be a human computer. So, he would amass stats, numbers on quarterbacks and then he would talk to pro coaches and pro scouts about the draftable quarterbacks. They would feed him information. I believe that often they hoodwinked Mel with bad quarterback info so that they could hide their interest in a certain quarterback and drive other pro teams who read Mel Kiper's reports away from the quarterback that they want. I honestly believe that Mel was used very often by pro teams to devalue a quarterback that they wanted so other teams would not draft him.

The true problem with draft experts talking about what college quarterback is going to be a good pro is that they use the external approach. It needs to be the internal approach. By this I mean in evaluating college quarterbacks for the pros they all use the same measuring board. How fast is he in the forty? How many times in the NFL does a quarterback ever run forty yards? Not many. How high can he jump? What the hell does that mean for an NFL quarterback? Or how far can a quarterback throw a football? How many times in a game does a quarterback throw a ball over 50 yards? Not many.

How tall is a quarterback? If he is 6'0 or under, he cannot play in Pro football, really?

These tests do not tell you about the really important things like how tough he is, can he stand in the pocket, take a hit, and deliver the football? Can he make quick decisions and how does he handle adversity? You won't find these key questions answered on any computer sheet. I would want to see a game film of a quarterback in games they lost by two or three or four touchdowns. Was that quarterback still playing hard, not giving up, trying to rally and inspire his teammates? You will not find those internal quarterback qualities on a stat sheet. You need the internal view over the external view.

Why it is important to look beyond the external measurables when you are evaluating a quarterback whether he be Black, White, Hispanic, or Asian. Two examples of incredible pro quarterbacks that would never have made a top of the draft board pick, but they had the internals, the things you couldn't see were: one, Doug Flutie out of Boston College and Brian Sipe of the Cleveland Browns.

The knock-on Doug Flutie was that he was too short. He could not see over the offensive line that was blocking for him or throw over the defensive linemen that were changing him. But the pro evaluators did not look inside the quarterback. His toughness, his leadership qualities were off the charts. His ability to make plays when there was nothing there. Flutie was a true creator. He played remarkable football for 21 years in pro football. Doug played 8 years in the Canadian Football League and 12 seasons in the NFL and one season in the USFL. Flutie was a 3-time Grey Cup Champion and a 3-time Grey Cup MVP. He holds the all-time CFL single season passing record with 6679 yards passing and 48 passing touchdowns in a single season. Think about those numbers for a moment, they are mind boggling staggering numbers. His all-time

NFL stats were 14,715 yards passing and 86 touchdowns. Eight years in the Canadian Football League and he threw for 41,355 yards, and rushed for 4,660 yards. Those numbers are so incredible you just have a difficult time wrapping your mind around them. But there was so much more to Doug Flutie than just numbers. He was excitement. He was energy. You knew that if you watched him closely play you would end up seeing a play that you have never seen before. Even though he was under 6' feet tall he could find windows to throw the ball over and around the behemoths trying to crush him. Flutie was the ultimate underdog. He played as if he was 6'6 and he put butts in the seats and eyeballs on the TV screen. He was an incredible football attraction. When he was at Boston College making remarkable plays like the Flutie "Hail Mary" against Miami he increased enrollment at Boston College. Enrollment went up 30% over Flutie's last wo years of amazing football at Boston College. And the Flutie Effect still lingers today and has helped smaller African American quarterbacks to be highly drafted and to be starting quarterbacks in the NFL, like Kyler Murray who is 5'10". He's a star African Amercian quarterback for the Cardinals. And the number one pick in the 2023 NFL April draft, African American quarterback Bryce Young, 5'10", who was the first pick in the NFL Draft for the Carolina Panthers. Without Flutie and him showing the (OWG) Old White Guys as coaches and owners that a 5'9" or 5'10" quarterback could star in the NFL. Doug Flutie made people rethink the position you, you did not have to be 6'4", 6'5", you could be 5'9" or 5'10", be mobile, creative and lead. That is the true and lasting Flutie effect on pro quarterbacks and helped to open the NFL door to smaller extremely mobile African American quarterbacks to get a real shot in the NFL. That is the lasting Flutie Effect for smaller mobile Black quarterbacks.

- TOM COLE -

DOUG FLUTIE
7
BUFFALO BILLS

Flutie's song is "Magic Man" by Heart. *"But try to understand, try to understand, try, try, try to understand, he's a magic man, mama, ah, he's a magic man"*

The second example I mentioned, even though there are so many evaluations you could question is Brian Sipe of the Cleveland Browns. Brian Sipe may have led for a couple of years the best, most exciting pro-offense in the history of pro football. The only one I would say is close to Sipe and his Kardiac Kids would be Dan Fouts and his San Diego Chargers or Montana and his 49ers. But Brian Sipe did his work in Cleveland with much less talent. Brian made it happen. Sipe was drafted in the 13th round of the 1972 NFL Draft by the Cleveland Brown. Brian sat for a number of years on the Cleveland Bench behind Mike Phipps. But when Sipe finally got a chance to become the true starter, the offensive explosion happened like none other in the history of pro football. Sipe created the "Kardiac Kids." From the 1979 and 1980 seasons Brian led the Browns to eight comebacks and eleven game-winning drives in the fourth quarter or overtime. Sipe was at his best when his back was against the wall and the clock was running down. The calm he had in the pocket and his ability to find open receivers in the most harried difficult situations was truly astonishing. There was no one like Sipe in the pocket with the game on the line, he was Errol Flynn in a Brown and Orange uniform, a swashbuckler in a number 17 Cleveland Browns jersey. He was always there to save the day as time ran out. In 1980 his NFL,

MVP season should have been a Cleveland Browns Super Bowl or as people in Cleveland were calling it the "Siper Bowl." If the weather in Cleveland wasn't 35 degress below with a wind chill, Sipe would have defeated the Oakland Raiders. He would have passed them silly. The brutal weather took the "Siper Bowl" away, But it will never take away the glorious memories of the 13th round draft pick out of San Diego, a surfer from the coast, who most have thought he was too short at 6'0 and too slight of build to play pro football. His years in Cleveland, Sipe threw for 23,713 yards and 154 touchdowns. There has never been any quarterback in Cleveland like the Kardiac Kid himself, Brian Sipe. Sipe like Flutie helped to open the door or kick the door in for smaller slight of build quarterbacks like the number one pick in the 2023 draft, Black quarterback Bryce Young out of Alabama.

BRIAN SIPE
17
CLEVELAND BROWNS

The Kardiac Kid gets a song by the Beach Boys called "Surfin' USA." *"If everybody had an ocean across the USA then everybody'd be surfin like California"*

A poem by Rudyard Kipling "IF" also reminds me of the Kardiac Kid. *"If you can meet with triumph and disaster and treat those two impostors just the same, if you can make one heap of all your winnings and risk it on one turn of a pitch and toss and lose, and start again at your beginnings and never breathe a word about your loss; if you can force your heart and nerve and sinew to serve your turn long after they are gone. And so, hold on when there is nothing in you except the will which says to them: Hold on!*

The Quarterback That Took a Knee

Colin Kaepernick was a 4.0 student in high school and a three-sport star athlete. He went to the University of Nevada. Colin maintained his 4.0 GPA in college and graduated with a degree in business. Colin became the only quarterback in D1 college football that in his career passed for 10,000 yards and rushed for 4000 yards. He was selected by the San Francisco 49ers in the second round of the 2011 draft.

In the middle of the 2012 San Francisco 49ers Football Season Kaepernick became a starter and led the San Franciso 49ers to the Super Bowl. In 2013 he helped the 49ers reach the NFC Championship Game. During the 49ers's third pre-season game in 2016 Colin Kaepernick sat on the San Francisco 49ers bench and did not stand for the National Anthem. Then for the following games during the anthem he just took a knee. This was Colin Kaepernick's personal protest against police brutality and a stand against racism in the United States. There was tremendous push back on Colin's taking a knee action during the National Anthem, on both views. There were many who thought Colin's actions disrespected the remarkable men and women that serve in our US military, also that it disrespected the incredibly brave men and women that have died or been injured defending our country and or Democracy and our way of life. Then there were many that said Colin had the right to protest. the right to speak up and that is a big part of the uniqueness of our very esoteric form of government, the best in the known world. Kaepernick received so many negative responses that the then President Donald Trump made a statement that the NFL owners should fire players who protest the National Anthem. This was coming from the same President that said John McCain, a heroic military man was not a war hero because he was captured and called him a loser for failing to win the Whitehouse in 2008. Eventually because of all of the push back on the National Anthem Colin was released by the San Francisco 49ers and no one else would give him an opportunity. Was there collusion among the other NFL owners. You would have to say yes.

Colin Kaepernick chose a peaceful form of protest to try to bring awareness to a difficult issue in the United States policing in our Black communities. As long as you are not endangering people for example, yelling "fire" in a crowded movie theater, you have the right to say and do things that you think are important to try to make our United States Democracy better. It is the best in the known world but not perfect. Sometimes it takes people speaking peacefully or protesting peacefully to keep improving our form of Democracy. I would think if you polled service men and women about the protest that Colin Kaepernick was doing during the National Anthem, many might not like it but they would defend his right to do it. That is what our incredibly brave men and women who serve every day to keep us safe are fighting for, the rights of United States Citizens to speak their minds, to peacefully protest, to worship as they please, to live where they like, to pursue any job that they are interested in and marry whomever they want. United States Democracy is Athens on a shinning hill. It is a true beacon of light of what a society can be. We are ever evolving, ever trying to get better but the uneducated nonsense of "America, love it or leave it" is a canard. It is not true. The United States Democracy is about speaking out when you see or hear injustice, because if any group of Americans are denied their right to peacefully protest or denied the right to speak out about injustice then we all lose our precious Democratic way of life.

COLIN KAEPERNICK
7
SAN FRANCISCO 49ERS

Colin's song is by the Beatles, and it's called "Revolution." *"You say you want a revolution, well, you know we all want to change the world, you tell me that it's evolution, well, you know we all want to change the world."*

The Day the Earth
Stood Still in Alabama

In 1970 an all-Black University of Southern California Trojan backfield, a quarterback, a full back, and a tail back beat the heck out of a segregated Alabama Team. It was the opening game of the 1970 football season at Alabama. Coach Bear Bryant was unwilling to integrate his Bama Team because of the segregation politics of the South. But he devised a plan with his good friend John McKay, head football coach at Southern California and drinking buddy, for McKay to bring his integrated team to Alabama and the segregated South. There were no Black players on the Alabama football team at that time. Sam the Bam Cunningham was an African American full back for Southern California in this opening game at Alabama. Sam had 12 carries for 135 yards and two touchdowns. Jimmy Jones was the Black quarterback and Clarence Davis the Black tailback for the University of Southern California. USC and their integrated football team destroyed Bear Bryant and his all-White Bama team 42-21. During that 1970 football season Jimmy Jones at Southern California passed for 1877 yards and 10 touchdowns. That same year Clarence Davis rushed for 1,175 yards and 11 touchdowns. This all-Black backfield of USC in 1970 that came to Legion Field in Alabama opened some white eyes. That game on September 12, 1970, helped to open people's minds to a new game of football. A more fair and equitable game of football which meant integration which was particularly important to the development of the southeast conference and Alabama. After that old fashioned butt kicking Coach Bryant felt free to play Wilbur Jackson who became the first African American football player at Alabama and then Alabama became the first team to integrate in the Southeastern Conference.

SAM BAM CUNNINGHAM
39
FULL BACK
USC

JIMMY JONES
8
QUARTERBACK
USC

CLARENCE DAVIS
28
USC

The song in honor of the 1970 All Black Backfield for USC and the first in the history of D1 football, is "Good Guys Don't Wear White" by the Standels. *"So tell your mama and your papa sometimes good guys don't wear white."*

The first all-Black backfield in the history of the Southeast Conference.

Dr. Arthur Carr
Ohio University

Dr. Arthur Carr was the first Black athlete and first Black quarterback in the history of Ohio University. Arthur Carr was an acclaimed athlete in high school and he went to Ohio University in 1903. Arthur may have been the first Black student to play football at a predominantly White university football team.

More important than his athletic contributions are Carr's legacy as a prominent African American in Athens, Ohio. Carr represents someone who is extremely important to the Ohio University Community and the surrounding Athens population. Arthur graduated from Ohio University in 1905 where he studied business. Carr then went on to study medicine at Howard University. Arthur graduated in 1912. He then moved to Richmond Virginia where he worked as a physician for nine years. He had an extremely successful career. Carr was able to go into White homes where no Black doctors have ever gone before in Athens. He was also made medical examiner for two large organizations in Richmond. In 1920 Arthur was named the President of the Association of African American Doctors.

Carr Hall was built in 2015 and named after Dr. Arthur Carr for student housing at Ohio University. Part of the Ohio University Football Stadium, Peden Stadium, was built on land that was donated by Arthur Carr's family. Dr. Carr's influence at Ohio University went way beyond being the first Black athlete and quarterback for the Bobcats.

His success, his remarkable talent and skills still influence and inspire students and faculty alike on the Campus of Ohio University today.

ARTHUR CARR
OHIO UNIVERSITY

They did not wear football numbers back in 1903 and 1904 so I cannot post his number, but a John F. Kennedy quote very much describes Dr. Arthur Carr better than any numbers ever could, *"One man can make a difference, and everyone should try"* Dr. Arthur Carr made a remarkable difference in sports and more importantly in life.

Thundering Herd

Reggie Oliver was the first starting quarterback in the history of Marshall University in 1971. Reggie threw the most important pass in Marshall University history. On September 25, 1971, the Thundering Herd was losing to Xavier 13-9 and Oliver threw a 13-yard game winning touchdown pass to give Marshall a 15-13 win in its first home game after the 1970 plane crash. Reggie did not go on the plane trip that crashed because he was a first-year student and freshman were ineligible to play according to NCAA rules at that time.

Reggie Oliver became the starting quarterback at Marshall for the next three years. After graduating from Marshall Reggie took a teaching and coaching position at Huntington High School. Oliver later became an assistant coach at Marshall under Sonny Randle and eventually became the head coach at Alabama A & M University and later at Eastmoor Academy in Columbus, Ohio. Oliver was inducted into the Marshall Athletic Hall of Fame in 1984.

Reggie Oliver, number 12, being the first Black quarterback in the history of Marshall University, stood up when his team and his school needed him most. He played under the most adverse conditions a quarterback can play, in a school that is rebuilding a program literally starting completely over. He helped put that team and that Marshall Community on his back to lift and rebuild a very storied program. Reggie Oliver's quarterback stats while he was at Marshall are 562 attempted passes and 240 completed passes for 2,886 yards and 13 touchdowns. Reggie stood very tall when his team and school needed him.

REGGIE OLIVER
12
MARSHALL UNIVERSITY

Reggie's song is by Alice Cooper called "Stand." *"You got style, and you got game, so get it out don't be ashamed, let everybody know your name, get it on out now, what's your name, yeah, stand up what do you believe in yeah stand up, come on."*

Penn State's First Black Quarterback

Mike Cooper in 1970 became the first Black starting quarterback for the Nittany Lions. Mike, in his first start, led the Penn State Nittany Lions to a 55-7 win over Navy on September 19, 1970. But then the Nittany Lions lost the next four games and Mike Cooper was replaced mid-season by future All-American John Hufnagel. Mike Cooper's stats at Penn State at the quarterback position were 61 completions and 121 attempts for 724 yards and 6 touchdowns passing. Cooper won the starting job at Penn State at quarterback during the Spring game in 1970. When Cooper was asked about being the first Black quarterback to start a Penn State Game, Cooper said, "I know I'm a good quarterback and a good athlete." Cooper also said he tries not to wear his bell bottoms around Coach Paterno, Coach loves to kid me about my mod clothes. It takes a great deal of confidence to play the quarterback position, but you also need a great deal of luck and talent around you. Unfortunately, Mike quarterbacked the next four games that were losses and he got replaced. When things are not going well the first person to go is the quarterback, the second is the head coach. But Mike Cooper can always rely on the fact, and no one can ever take it away from him, that he was the first Black quarterback in the history of Penn State. He is a big part of the school history and led the way for other African American quarterbacks at Penn State like Wally Richardson number 14 in the Penn State program.

Wally was a two-year starter at quarterback under Coach Paterno at Penn State. Wally Richardson led the Nittany Lions to a 20-5 record and victories in the 1996 Outback Bowl and the 1997 Fiesta Bowl. In those games Wally threw for 312 yards and 5 touchdowns. A co-captain of the 1996 squad Richardson ranks second in school history in single game with 33 completions. Following his senior year Wally received the Ridge Riley Award which honors a senior lettered athlete for sportsmanship, scholarship, leadership, and friendship. Wally Richardson was a four time Academic All-Big Ten selection; he compiled a 3.2 GPA in administration of Justice.

Wally played a little professional football but after his retirement from football Richardson joined Penn State's Morgan Academic Support Center for student athletes, first as a graduate assistant in 2001 and then as an academic counselor from 2003 to 2007. From 2007 to 2011 Wally served as an associate director for the University of Georgia. He worked with members of the football team, women's volleyball, and equestrian teams. Wally was then named associate director of football for the University of North Carolina for the 2011 season. In April of 2013 Richardson was named director of the Penn State Football Letterman's Club. Wally's impact and influence was large, he was a true role model for other Penn State student athletes.

MIKE COOPER
25
PENN STATE

Mike's song is "Bell Bottom Blues" by Eric Clapton. *"Bell Bottom Blues you made me cry."*

His Head Coach Joe Paterno did not like the "Bell Bottoms." If you can remember seeing Coach Joe Paterno on the sideline in his football attire, you might think Joe could have upgraded his look in "Bell Bottoms."

WALLY RICHARDSON
14
PENN STATE

Wally's song is "Can't You Hear Me Knocking" by the Rolling Stones. *"Can't you hear me knocking on your window, can't you hear me knocking at your door, can't you hear me knocking."*

Wally Richardson really did kick the door down for African American quarterbacks at Penn State.

It isn't Easy

65

Through the 1960's, 1970's and 1980's so very often African American quarterbacks were asked to change positions once they got to the NFL. That is not easy to do. Let's say you are asked to become a running back. Running the ball up inside the offensive line or running around end are totally different than running the ball from the pocket out of a scramble. First of all, you have the opportunity running from the pocket as a quarterback to get down and land the plane on the ground so to speak before some salivating defensive player has the opportunity to really put a "slobberknocker" hit on you. If they try to switch a quarterback to a safety position, the quarterback moved to safety may have a great knowledge of passing routes. There are only so many cuts former quarterbacks may be able to recognize quickly having played quarterback. The real problem is when the quarterback turned safety has to come up, square up and tackle a 245-pound running back attacking him at full speed. Quarterbacks are not used to tackling. The most difficult transition the Black quarterback was asked to do is to become a wide receiver. Throwing the football and catching the football are two very different fundamental motions. Because someone is a gifted quarterback does not necessarily follow that they would have the required speed that you need to play at wide receiver in the NFL to separate from defenses. You could have excellent speed for a quarterback, run 4.6 or 4.7 in the 40-yard dash but that same speed at a wide receiver in the NFL will not separate you from anyone else.

Learning to keep your head still while you are running a route is a skill that is difficult to acquire.

Quarterback is such a unique position in sports, but the skills you need to have to play that position successfully in the NFL are not skills that are easily transferred to other football positions in the NFL. It is much easier to make those kind of quarterback switches to other positions vis a vie, safety, wide receiver, running back in high school or college, still not easy but easier. In the NFL, those kind of quarterback position switches are so very hard to do in the NFL, trying to switch a quarterback to another position is a zero sum game. The quarterback that wins the competition will be fine, the quarterback that loses the competition might not be able to play another position. Now there are pro football followers that will give you examples of quarterback switches that worked, there are a few but these are anomalies. Marlin Briscoe did it, but he was one of the very few that could do it and do it successfully, as a matter-of-fact Marlin made it to the Super Bowl at wide receiver, but he is truly an exception. He was just a superior athlete; most do not make it.

Tip of the helmet to all the college quarterbacks that tried to make the NFL playing another position. As Ringo Starr of the Beatles once said, "It Don't Come Easy."

In Case You were Wondering

66

In case you were wondering, the first White quarterback to play football at an all-Black College, Grambling University, was Jim Gregory. The legendary football Coach, one of the greatest of all time, Coach Eddie Robinson thought it would be important for his all-Black team to experience integration in a unique way. He brought Jim Gregory, a White quarterback and kicker to integrate his team. The great Eddie Robinson felt that his players would learn to know a White player, become friends with a White player and more importantly accept Jim Gregory as part of the Grambling Team. Jim played 60 seconds of quarterback time because he was playing behind the phenomenal quarterback James Harris that we profiled in depth in "Black in the Pocket." As a matter of fact, James Harris and Jim Gregory became very good friends. A major motion picture was made about the Jim Gregory Story at Grambling University, the movie was called, "The White Tiger." Jim Gregory graduated from Grambling and has had a remarkable teaching and coaching career in high school for thirty years. He also uses the movie about himself, Coach Robinson, James Harris, and the rest of the outstanding Grambling Football team to talk about race and how important that it is to try to understand one another and how important it is to try to come together as a people as a society. Coach Eddie Robinson, quarterback James Harris, quarterback Jim Gregory and the rest of the Grambling Team did that very thing, they came together, liked, and respected one another and taught valuable lessons to all of us.

JIM GREGORY

12

GRAMBLING UNIVERSITY

The song that reminds me of Jim's time at Grambling University is "Get Together" by the Youngbloods. *"Come on people now smile on your brother, everybody get together, try to love one another right now."*

Epilogue

Black in the Pocket is a book that hopes to create an awareness of the struggle that Black quarterbacks went through in the 1960's, 1970's and 1980's to try to create a level playing field to have a fair opportunity to play and compete. It is important to help people understand how difficult those particular paths were. It is also important, I believe, to honor the coaches that saw through the racism and gave fair and equal opportunity.

The incredible Black quarterbacks today in Professional Football have stood on the shoulders of many that came before them. We tried to tell those stories. America has always been about opportunity. Currently in the NFL there are 14 starting African American quarterbacks playing in the NFL. Two African American quarterbacks started in the Super Bowl in 2023. Remarkable progress has been made due certainly in part to the coaches and Black quarterbacks we profile in Black in the Pocket. The hope is as we move forward, a quarterback will no longer be a "Black Quarterback" but just a "Quarterback." I hope you enjoyed the journey reading *Black in the Pocket* and I hope everyone keeps their eyes downfield looking for fairness, respect, and dignity.

Postscript

Our grandson, Cooper Hemke is 9 years old and is a big time NFL fan and a true Patrick Mahomes supporter. Cooper does not care whether Mahomes is Black, White, Hispanic, or Asian. He genuinely likes Mahomes because he is an incredibly exciting quarterback that leads his team and makes truly thrilling plays. He wears his Mahomes jersey most days. Now his mom, Christy Cole Hemke, a magistrate, and his dad, Sam Hemke, a Senior Market Field Manager, are Cooper's real heroes but in his life Patrick Mahomes No. 15 is also important.

We have come along way now, Patrick Mahomes is not a Black Quarterback, he is just "Mahomes" and isn't that the way it should be!

Drawn by Cooper Hemke

Acknowledgements

This book would not have happened without my wife, Karen. She brought tremendous skill, direction, organization, and insight. Thank you honey. Our son Clayton Cole did a number of the AI generated photos we used in the book and helped give it a fresh look. We love you, Clay. Our granddaughter Josie Hemke drew a picture of Marlin Briscoe and our grandson Cooper Hemke drew a picture of Mahomes.

Nick Marconi took our idea for a cover for Black in the Pocket and made it a reality. He's a good artist in his own right. Tom Peyton, a college friend, also gave us information on using AI photos and we used several that he produced in this book.

Many thanks to the incredible work that Melanie Lear from AuthorHouse did on our book *Black in the Pocket*.

Lastly, thank you to all the outstanding African American Quarterbacks who created these remarkable stories and moved our country forward.

Notes

Chapter 2 – Marlin Briscoe – Pro Football History.com Jon Kendle, Pro Football History.com, The Making of the Magician by Ben Swanson, Wikipedia.com, Associated Press, Broncos.com Ben Swanson

Chapter 3 – James Harris – American Football Data Base.com, Jake Elman, Martin Luther King

Chapter 4 – Chuck Ealey – Kirk Heidelberg

Chapter 5 – Joe Gilliam – Wikipedia

Chapter 6 – Doug Williams – The History Makers

Chapter 7 – The Duke and Kenny Washington – Pro Football.com, African American Registry, personal conversations with Bob Snyder.

Chapter 8 – Coaches that Broke the Black Ceiling – K. Frank@The Blade.com, Tom Shanahan.report

Chapter 10 – Every Starting African Quarterback in Pro Football – Wikipedia.com

Chapter 13 – Warren Moon – American Football Data Base, Wikipedia

Chapter 14 – Andre Ware – Wikipedia

Chapter 16 – Doug Williams – New York Times

Chapter 18 – Michael Vick – Pro Football Network

Chapter 19 – The Beatles – BBC.com, Yahoo.news

Chapter 20 – Sonny Sixkiller – Wikipedia

Chapter 21 – Donovan McNabb – Fanbuzz.com

Chapter 22 – Lombardi Stands Up – Wikipedia.com

Chapter 25 – Doug & Joe – Washington Post.com

Chapter 26 – Michigan State Helped Lead the Way – Fox Sports.com, Austin Chronicle.com

Chapter 27 – One Man's View – Austin Chronicle.com

Chapter 28 – Hayden Fry – Wikipedia

Chapter 30 – The Tide Could Have Turned Early – Wikipedia.com

Chapter 31 – Cornelius Greene – American Football Data Base

Chapter 32 – Dennis Franklin – Wikipedia.com

Chapter 33 – Cliff Brown, Wikipedia.com

Chapter 34 – Tony Rice – Wikipedia.com

Chapter 36 – First Black Quarterback in CFL – Wikipedia.com

Chapter 37 – Black Quarterbacks Hit Gold in Canada – Canadian Football and Landscape.com

Chapter 40 – Warren Moon – Wikipedia.com, American Football Database

Chapter 61 – Dr. Arthur Carr – Athen News.com

Chapter 62 – Thundering Herd – Herdzone.com

Chapter 63 – Penn State's First Black Quarterback – Blackhistory.psu.edu, Football Foundation.org

Chapter 65 – In Case You Were Wondering – Gramblingblogspot.com

Author's Bio

Tom Cole was the first quarterback at St. John's Jesuit High School. He played quarterback at Ohio Wesleyan University and majored in History with a minor in English. He taught and coached in High School and college. In football he coached quarterbacks and was offensive coordinator.

He also was a TV Sports Broadcaster on Buckeye Cable and the Buckeye Cable Sports Network for 26 years, broadcasting MAC Football and Basketball on BCSN and ESPN III. He also did over 10,000 interviews on the BCSN Network.

He is currently the Community Outreach Coordinator for the Taylor Automotive Family.

Cole is also in the City of Toledo Athletic Hall of Fame and the St. John's Jesuit High School Hall of Fame.

Cole has won 7 Ohio Cable TV Broadcast Awards, plus he was named MVP at BCSN.

Black in the Pocket is his fourth sports book.

Tomcole1717@gmail.com
419-870-1931

Printed in the United States
by Baker & Taylor Publisher Services